Ivy Global

ISEE MIDDLE LEVEL TESTS

1ST EDITION

IVY GLOBAL, NEW YORK

*ISEE is a registered trademark of the Educational Records Bureau which is not affiliated with and does not endorse this product.
This publication was written and edited by the team at Ivy Global.

Editors: Corwin Henville and Laurel Perkins
Layout Editor: Sacha Azor
Contributors: Sarah Atkins, Ali Candib, Tamara Jordan, Nathan Létourneau, Sarah Pike, and Julia Romanski
Producers: Lloyd Min and Junho Suh

About Ivy Global

Ivy Global is a pioneering education company that provides a wide range of educational services.

E-mail: info@ivyglobal.com
Website: http://www.ivyglobal.com

CONTENTS

INTRODUCTION

CHAPTER 1

HOW TO USE THIS BOOK

SECTION 1

Welcome, students and parents! This book is intended for students practicing for the Middle Level Independent School Entrance Exam (ISEE). For students applying to many top private and independent schools in North America, the ISEE is a crucial and sometimes daunting step in the admissions process. By exposing you to the format of the ISEE, Ivy Global will help you build your confidence and maximize your score on this important exam.

This book is right for you if:

- you are applying to a private or independent school that requires the ISEE for admission
- you will be in Grades 6-7 when you take the ISEE
- you would like to practice for the ISEE exam using full-length practice tests under simulated testing conditions
- you are a parent, family member, or tutor looking for new ways to help your Middle Level ISEE student

We know that no two students are exactly alike—each student brings a unique combination of personal strengths and weaknesses to his or her test preparation. For this reason, we've tailored our preparation materials to help students with a specific subject area or goal.

Ivy Global's *ISEE English* includes the best strategies for the ISEE Verbal Reasoning and Reading Comprehension sections, plus a step-by-step approach to the Essay section and a thorough vocabulary and writing skills review.

Ivy Global's *ISEE Math* includes the best strategies for the ISEE Quantitative Reasoning and Mathematics Achievement sections, plus thorough review and practice for all of the math concepts tested at each level.

Ivy Global's products are available for purchase at ivyglobal.com/products or amazon.com.

This book includes:

- an up-to-date introduction to the ISEE's administration, format, and scoring practices
- instructions for taking a full-length practice test for the ISEE under simulated testing conditions
- 2 full-length practice tests for the ISEE Middle Level
- detailed scoring instructions for the exam

To make the best use of this book, take time to assess your strengths and weaknesses after you have worked through an exam. Then, spend some time reviewing the concepts you found challenging before you test yourself again.

To get started, continue reading for an overview of the ISEE. Good luck in this exciting new step for your education!

ABOUT THE ISEE

SECTION 2

The **ISEE (Independent School Entrance Exam)** is a standardized test administered to students in grades 1-11 to help determine placement into certain private and independent schools. Many secondary schools worldwide use the ISEE as an integral part of their admissions process. The ISEE is owned and published by the Educational Records Bureau.

You will register for one of four ISEE tests, depending on your grade level:

- The **Primary Level** exam is for students currently in grades 1-3.
- The **Lower Level** exam is for students currently in grades 4-5.
- The **Middle Level** exam is for students currently in grades 6-7.
- The **Upper Level** exam is for students currently in grades 8-11.

The Primary Level exam is administered only with the use of a computer, and includes auditory content. All other levels may be taken on a computer or in a paper-and-pencil format. Among levels, the exams differ in difficulty, length, and the types of questions that may appear. The Lower Level exam is shorter than the Middle or Upper level exams.

WHEN IS THE TEST ADMINISTERED?

Administration dates for the ISEE vary between test locations. ISEE test sites and administration dates can be found online, at ERBlearn.org. In addition to taking the test at a school that administers large group tests, students applying to grades 5-12 can register to take the ISEE at a Prometric Testing Center, which administers computer-based exams.

HOW MANY TIMES CAN I TAKE THE TEST?

Students may only take the ISEE once per admission season. The version of the test doesn't matter: a student who has taken a paper-and-pencil test may not take another test on a computer, and a student who has taken a computer-based test may not take another test in a paper-and-pencil format.

HOW DO I REGISTER?

The easiest and fastest way to register is to complete the **online application**. Visit www.ERBlearn.org to register for an exam in your area. It is also possible to register over the phone by calling (800) 446-0320 or (919) 956-8524, or to register by mail. To register by mail, you must complete and submit the application form available only in the printed ISEE student guide. Visit www.ERBlearn.org to order a printed copy of the ISEE student guide.

WHAT IS THE FORMAT OF THE ISEE?

The Lower, Middle, and Upper Level ISEE exams consist of four scored sections (**Verbal Reasoning**, **Quantitative Reasoning**, **Reading Comprehension**, and **Mathematics Achievement**), plus an **Essay** that is used as a writing sample. The format of the test differs based on the level of the exam:

LOWER LEVEL			
Section	**Questions**	**Length**	**Topics Covered**
Verbal Reasoning	34	20 min	Synonyms, Sentence Completion
Quantitative Reasoning	38	35 min	Logical Reasoning, Pattern Recognition (Word Problems)
Reading Comprehension	25	25 min	Short Passages
Math Achievement	30	30 min	Arithmetic, Algebra, Geometry, Data Analysis
Essay	1	30 min	One age-appropriate essay prompt
Total testing time: 2 hours 20 minutes			

MIDDLE AND UPPER LEVEL			
Section	**Questions**	**Length**	**Topics Covered**
Verbal Reasoning	40	20 min	Synonyms, Sentence Completion
Quantitative Reasoning	37	35 min	Logical Reasoning, Pattern Recognition (Word Problems and Quantitative Comparison)
Reading Comprehension	36	35 min	Short Passages
Math Achievement	47	40 min	Arithmetic, Algebra, Geometry, Data Analysis
Essay	1	30 min	One age-appropriate essay prompt
Total testing time: 2 hours 40 minutes			

Except for the Essay, all questions are **multiple-choice** (A) to (D). You are not normally allowed to use calculators, rulers, dictionaries, or other aids during the exam. However, students with documented learning disabilities or physical challenges may apply to take the test with extra time, aids, or other necessary accommodations that they receive in school. For more information about taking the ISEE with a documented disability, visit the ISEE Website at ERBlearn.org.

HOW IS THE ISEE SCORED?

All of the multiple-choice questions on the ISEE are equal in value, and your **raw score** for these sections is the total number of questions answered correctly. There is no penalty for incorrect answers.

Within each section, there are also 5-6 **experimental questions** that do not count towards your raw score for the section. The ISEE uses these questions to measure exam accuracy and to test material for upcoming exams. You won't be told which questions are the experimental questions, however, so you have to do your best on the entire section.

Your raw score for each section is then converted into a **scaled score** that represents how well you did in comparison to other students who have taken the same exam. Scaled scores range from about 760-950 for each section, with total scaled scores ranging from about 2280-2850.

The **Essay** is not scored, but is sent to the schools you are applying to as a sample of your writing skills. Admissions officers may use your essay to evaluate your writing ability when they are making admissions decisions.

Scores are released to families, and to the schools that families have designated as recipients, within 7-10 business days after the test date. Scores will be mailed to the address you provided when registering for the ISEE, and to up to six schools and/or counselors. You may request expedited score reports, or send score reports to additional schools or counselors, for an additional fee.

WHAT ARE THE ISEE PERCENTILES AND STANINES?

The ISEE score report also provides **ISEE percentile** rankings for each category, comparing your performance to that of other students in the same grade who have taken the test in the past three years. If you score in the 60th percentile, this means you are scoring higher than 60% of other students in your grade taking the exam.

These percentile rankings provide a more accurate way of evaluating student performance at each grade level. However, the ISEE percentiles are a comparison against only other students who have taken the ISEE, and these tend to be very high-achieving students. Students should not be discouraged if their percentile rankings appear low.

The following chart shows the median (50th percentile) ISEE scores for students applying to grades 5-12.

MEDIAN SCORES (ISEE 50TH PERCENTILE) FOR 2012					
Level	**Grade Applying To**	**Verbal Reasoning**	**Quantitative Reasoning**	**Reading Comprehension**	**Mathematics Achievement**
Lower Level	5	840	843	834	848
	6	856	856	848	863
Middle Level	7	863	865	866	871
	8	869	871	871	876
Upper Level	9	879	878	880	882
	10	883	882	886	886
	11	886	885	889	890
	12	881	884	880	889

The ISEE score report also includes **stanine** rankings. A stanine is a number from 1-9 obtained by dividing the entire range of students' scores into 9 segments, as shown in the table below:

percentile rank	stanine
1 – 3	1
4 – 10	2
11 – 22	3
23 – 39	4
40 – 59	5
60 – 76	6
77 – 88	7

89 – 95	8
96 – 99	9

Stanine scores are provided because small differences in percentile rankings may not represent a significant difference in ability. Stanines represent a range of percentile rankings, and are intended to provide a better representation of student ability.

HOW DO SCHOOLS USE THE ISEE?

Schools use the ISEE as one way to assess potential applicants, but it is by no means the only tool that they are using. Schools also pay very close attention to the rest of a student's application—academic record, teacher recommendations, extracurricular activities, writing samples, and interviews—in order to determine which students might be the best fit for their program. The personal components of a student's application sometimes give schools a lot more information about the student's personality and potential contributions to the school's overall community. Different schools place a different amount of importance on ISEE and other test scores within this process, and admissions offices are good places to find out how much your schools of interest will weight the ISEE.

TEST-TAKING STRATEGIES

CHAPTER 2

APPROACHING THE ISEE

SECTION 1

Before you review the content covered on the ISEE, you need to focus on *how* you take the ISEE. If you approach the ISEE *thoughtfully* and *strategically*, you will avoid common traps and tricks planted in the ISEE by the test makers. Think of the ISEE as a timed maze—you need to make every turn cleverly and quickly so that you avoid getting stuck at a dead end with no time to spare.

In this section, you will learn about the ISEE's format and structure; this awareness will help you avoid any surprises or shocks on test day. The ISEE is a very predictable exam and will seem less challenging once you understand what it looks like and how it works. By learning and practicing the best test-taking strategies and techniques, you will discover how to work as quickly and efficiently as possible. Once you know what to expect, you can refine your knowledge of the actual material tested on the ISEE, such as the verbal and math skills that are based on your grade level in school.

This section on ISEE strategies will answer the following **major questions**:

1. How does the ISEE differ from a test you take in school?
2. What preparation strategies can you learn before you take the ISEE?
3. What strategies can you learn to use during the ISEE?
4. How can you manage stress before and during the ISEE?

In the process of answering your big questions, this section will also highlight key facts about smart test-taking:

- Your answer choice matters—your process does not. Enter your answer choices correctly and carefully to earn points. You have a set amount of time per section, so spend it wisely.
- The ISEE's format and directions do not change, so learn them now.
- All questions have the same value.
- Each level of the ISEE corresponds to a range of grades, and score expectations differ based on your grade level.
- Identify your areas of strength and weakness, and review any content that feels unfamiliar.

- Apply universal strategies—prediction-making, Process of Elimination, back-solving, and educated guessing—to the multiple-choice sections.
- Stay calm and be confident in your abilities as you prepare for and take the ISEE.

HOW DOES THE ISEE DIFFER FROM A TEST YOU TAKE IN SCHOOL?

The ISEE differs from tests you take in school in four major ways:

1. It is not concerned with the process behind your answers. Your answer is either right or wrong: there is no partial credit.
2. You have a set amount of time per section (and for the exam as a whole).
3. It is divided into four levels that correspond to four grade ranges of students.
4. It is extremely predictable given that its format, structure, and directions never vary.

NO PARTIAL CREDIT

At this point in your school career, you have probably heard your teacher remark, "Be sure to show your work on the test!" You are most likely familiar with almost every teacher's policy of "No work, no credit." However, the ISEE completely ignores this guideline. The machine that grades your exam does not care that you penciled brilliant logic in the margins of the test booklet—the machine only looks at your answer choice. Your answer choice is either right or wrong: **there is no partial credit**.

SET AMOUNT OF TIME

You have a **set amount of time per section**, so spend it wisely. The ISEE test proctors will never award you extra time after a test section has ended because you spent half of one section struggling valiantly on a single problem. Instead, you must learn to work within each section's time constraints.

You also must view the questions as equal because **each question is worth the same number of points** (one). Even though some questions are more challenging than others, they all carry the same weight. Rather than dwell on a problem, you should skip it, work through the rest of the section, and come back to it if you have time.

FOUR LEVELS

There are four levels of the ISEE—Primary, Lower, Middle, and Upper—each of which is administered to a specific range of students. The Primary Level is given to students applying to grades 2, 3, and 4; the Lower Level is given to students applying to grades 5 and 6; the Middle Level is given to students applying to grades 7 and 8; and the Upper Level is given to students applying to grades 9, 10, 11, and 12. While you might be used to taking tests in school that are completely tailored to your grade, the ISEE is different: each test level covers content for a specific range of grade levels.

Score expectations differ based on your grade level. You are not expected to answer every question correctly on an Upper Level exam if you are only in eighth grade. Conversely, if you are in eleventh grade, you are expected to answer the most questions correctly on the Upper Level exam because you are one of the oldest students taking that exam.

STANDARD FORMAT

The ISEE is, by definition, a **standardized test**, which means that its format and directions are standard and predictable. While your teachers might change formats and directions for every assessment they administer, you can expect to see the same format and directions on every ISEE.

WHAT PREPARATION STRATEGIES CAN YOU LEARN BEFORE YOU TAKE THE ISEE?

Now that you are familiar with how the ISEE differs from the tests you take in school, you are ready to learn some test tips. You can prepare for the ISEE by following these three steps:

1. Learn the format and directions of the test.
2. Identify your areas of strength and weakness.
3. Create a study schedule to review and practice test content.

LEARN THE FORMAT AND DIRECTIONS

The structure of the ISEE is entirely predictable, so learn this now. Rather than wasting precious time reading the directions and understanding the format on test day, take the time now to familiarize yourself with the test's format and directions.

Refer to the tables on pages 6 and 7 for an overview of the ISEE's format. Continue reading for specific directions for the Verbal Reasoning, Reading Comprehension, and Essay sections. Specific directions for the Quantitative Reasoning and Mathematics Achievement sections can be found in Ivy Global's *ISEE Math*.

IDENTIFY YOUR STRENGTHS AND WEAKNESSES

To determine your areas of strength and weakness and to get an idea of which concepts you need to review, take a full-length, accurate practice exam to serve as a diagnostic test. Practice exams for the ISEE can be found in this book.

Make sure you simulate test day conditions by timing yourself. Then, check your answers against the correct answers. Write down how many questions you missed in each section, and note the topics or types of questions you found most challenging. What was hard about the test? What did you feel good about? Did you leave a lot of questions blank because of timing issues, or did you leave questions blank because you did not know how to solve them? Reflecting on these questions, in addition to looking at your score breakdown, will help you determine your strengths, weaknesses, and areas for improvement.

CREATE A STUDY SCHEDULE

After determining your areas of strength and weakness, create a study plan and schedule for your ISEE preparation to review content. Work backward from your test date until you arrive at your starting point for studying. The number of weeks you have until your exam will determine how much time you can (and should) devote to your preparation. Remember, practice is the most important thing!

To begin, try using this sample study plan as a model for your own personalized study schedule.

SAMPLE STUDY PLAN

My test date is: _________________.

I have ____ weeks to study. I will make an effort to study ____ minutes/hours each night, and I will set aside extra time on _________________ to take timed sections.

I plan to take ____ full-length tests between now and my test date. I will study for ____ weeks and then take a practice test. My goal for this test is to improve my score in the following sections:

____

____

____

____

____

____

____

____

If I do not make this goal, then I will spend more time studying.

STUDY SCHEDULE				
Date	**Plan of Study**	**Time Allotted**	**Time Spent**	**Goal Reached?**
1/1	Learn 5 words and review perimeter of polygons	1 hour	44 minutes	Yes, I know 5 new words and can calculate perimeter!
1/3	Learn 5 words and review area of triangles	1 hour	1 hour	I know 5 new words, but I'm still confused about the area of triangles. I'll review this again next time and ask a teacher, tutor, or parent for help.

WHAT STRATEGIES CAN YOU LEARN TO USE DURING THE TEST?

Once you have grown accustomed to the ISEE through practice, you are ready to learn strategies to use during the ISEE. The following points will prepare you to take the test as cleverly and efficiently as possible:

1. Enter your answer choices correctly and carefully.
2. Pace yourself to manage your time effectively.
3. Learn a strategic approach for multiple-choice questions.

ENTERING ANSWER CHOICES

Whether you are taking a pencil-and-paper or a computer-based exam, you must follow the directions carefully to enter your answers. In school you probably take tests that, for the most part, do not ask you to enter your answers in a specific format. However, the ISEE streamlines the grading process by only reviewing the answers you have entered on your answer sheet or into the computer program. This means that any notes or work you have written on your scratch paper will not be reviewed, and you will only receive credit for entering your answers correctly.

On a computer-based exam, you will click an answer on the computer screen in order to enter your response. Follow the directions carefully to make sure your answer has been recorded. Within each section, you will be able to go back to questions earlier in the section and change your answers. You will also be able to skip questions and come back to them later. However, you will not be able to review questions from sections that come earlier or later in the exam; you will only be able to review your answers for the questions in the section you are currently working on. Make sure all of your answers have been entered correctly before your time is up for the section.

On a pencil-and-paper exam, you will enter your answers on a separate answer sheet. You must grid in your multiple-choice answers onto this sheet using an HB pencil to fill in the circle that corresponds to your answer. This sheet is scanned and scored by a highly sensitive computer. You will also write your Essay on separate lined pages of this answer sheet.

Since you have to take an additional step to record your answers, it is important that you avoid making gridding mistakes. Sadly, many students get confused and mismark their answer sheets. Remember, even if you arrive at the right answer, it is only correct and counted in your favor if you grid correctly on your answer sheet.

To grid correctly and carefully to maximize your points, consider the following tips:

Keep your answer sheet neat. Since your answer sheet is graded by a machine, your score is calculated based on what your marks look like. The machine cannot know what you really meant if you picked the wrong bubble. Stray marks can harm your score, especially if you darken the correct answer but accidentally make a mark that confuses the machine! Avoid this and other errors by consulting the following image, which shows the difference between answers that are properly shaded and those that are not.

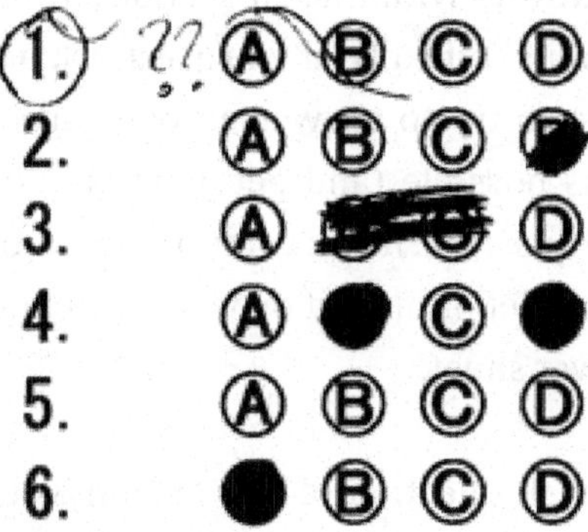

Answer 1 is *wrong* because no answer is selected and there are stray marks.
Answer 2 is *wrong* because choice (D) has not been darkened completely.
Answer 3 is *wrong* because two answers have been partially selected.
Answer 4 is *wrong* because two answers have been selected.
Answer 5 is *neither right nor wrong* because it was left blank.
Answer 6 is *right* because choice (A) has been darkened properly.

Train yourself to **circle your answer choice in your test booklet**. If you have time to go back and check your answers, you can easily check your circled answers against your gridded ones.

You should also **create a system for marking questions that you skipped** or that you found confusing (see the next section for more information about skipping questions). Try circling those question numbers only in your test booklet so that you can find them later if you want to solve them or check your work. Be aware of these questions when gridding answers on your answer sheet.

Finally, **grid your answers in batches of four, five, or six answer choices.** That way, you do not have to go back and forth between your test booklet and your answer sheet every minute. If you choose to use this strategy, keep an eye on the clock—you do not want to get to the end of the section and find you have not gridded any answers. Depending on how much time you have left to check your work (if you happen to finish early), you can either review every problem or spot-check a series of questions on your answer sheet against your test booklet.

TIME MANAGEMENT (PACING)

Manage your time effectively to boost your score. The ISEE has an element of time pressure, so it is important to keep moving on the exam rather than spending too much time on any single question.

You can come back to questions within each section of the ISEE. Each question is only worth one point, regardless of its difficulty. If you are stuck on a problem, you should make your best guess and move on to try to answer another problem. It makes more sense to answer as many questions as possible (and get as many points as possible) rather than spending all your time on one question. If you come across a question you want to come back to, circle it in your question booklet or mark it on your scratch paper. Remember not to make any stray marks on your answer sheet.

By moving quickly through each question of the section, you will ensure that: 1) you see every question in the section; 2) you gain points on questions that are easy for you; 3) you return to more challenging problems and figure out as many as you can with your remaining time. It is also important to note that you might not be able to answer several questions in each section if you are on the younger end of the testing group for your particular test level. In that case, you should make your best guess based on the information you do know, but shouldn't worry if the content is unfamiliar.

Even if you are unsure about a question and want to come back to it later, you should **always make a guess.** The ISEE doesn't take off any points for answering questions incorrectly, so you should never leave a question blank! Even if you guess a completely random answer, you have a small chance of gaining a point. If you can rule out one or two choices that you know are wrong, you have even better odds of guessing the right answer. Therefore, always make a guess on every question, even if you are planning to come back to it later. When your time is up, you want to make sure that you have entered an answer for every question!

Follow this step-by-step process for moving through a section:

1. Look through the section and answer the questions that are easy for you. If a question seems difficult or is taking too long, make a guess and circle it to come back to later.
2. After answering all the easier questions, go back to the questions you have circled and spend some time working on ones that you think you might be able to solve. If you figure out that the answer you originally guessed was incorrect, change that answer on your answer sheet.
3. If you have no idea how to solve a question, leave your best guess as your answer.
4. If you have any time remaining, check your work for the questions you solved.

STRATEGIES FOR MULTIPLE-CHOICE QUESTIONS

Apply universal strategies—prediction-making, Process of Elimination, back-solving, and educated guessing—to the multiple-choice sections. To illustrate the value of these strategies, read through the following example of a synonym question from the Verbal Reasoning section:

HAPPY:

(A) delighted

(B) unhappy

(C) crazy

(D) nice

Answer: (A). "Delighted" is the correct answer because it is the word that most nearly means "happy."

Regardless of whether the answer choices are easy, difficult, or somewhere in between, you can use certain tricks and tips to your advantage. To approach ISEE questions effectively, you need to step into the test makers' minds and learn to avoid their traps.

Make predictions. When you see a question, try to come up with an answer on your own before looking at the answer choices. You can literally cover the answer choices with your hand so that you must rely on your own intelligence to predict an answer instead of being swayed by answer choices that you see. If you look at the answer choices first, you might be tempted to pick an answer without thinking about the other options and what the question is asking you. Instead, make a prediction so that you understand the question fully and get a clear sense of what to look for in the answers. In the synonym example above, you could predict that a possible synonym for "happy" would be something like "glad."

Use the Process of Elimination. For each multiple-choice question, you must realize that the answer is right in front of you. To narrow down your answer choices, think about the potential incorrect answers and actively identify those to eliminate them. Even if you can eliminate just one answer, you will set yourself up for better odds if you decide to guess. For the synonym example above, test your prediction of "glad" against the answer choices and immediately eliminate "unhappy" since it is opposite in meaning. You can also probably eliminate "crazy" and "nice" since those words do not match your prediction. This leaves you with "delighted," which is the correct answer.

Try back-solving. This strategy is most useful on the math sections, especially when you are given a complicated, multi-step word problem. Instead of writing an equation, try plugging in the answer choices to the word problem. Take a look at the following question:

Catherine has a basket of candy. On Monday, she eats ½ of all the candy. On Tuesday, she eats 2 pieces. On Wednesday, she eats twice the amount of candy that she consumed on Tuesday. If she only has 4 pieces left on Thursday, how many pieces did she initially have?

(A) 12

(B) 14

(C) 16

(D) 20

To use back-solving, start with answer choice (C) and plug it into the word problem. If (C) is the correct answer, you are done. If not, you will then know whether you should test (B) or (D). When we start with 16 pieces of candy, we subtract 8 on Monday, then 2 more for Tuesday, and then 4 more for Wednesday. By Thursday, Catherine only has two pieces of candy left, which is less than the amount we wanted. Therefore, we know our answer has to be bigger, so we eliminate choices (A), (B), and (C) and try (D), which works.

(*Fun Fact:* If you think about it, you will have to plug in three answer choices at most to determine the right answer.)

Armed with these strategies, you might feel that the ISEE is starting to look more manageable because you now have shortcuts that will help you navigate the maze of questions quickly and cleverly.

Take a look at this example to practice using the strategies you just read about.

Because Kaitlin was -------- from her soccer game, she went to bed early.

(A) thrilled

(B) exhausted

(C) competitive

(D) inspired

1. Assess the question and recognize what it is testing. In this case, the question tests whether you can pick a word to complete the sentence.
2. Make a prediction. What about Kaitlin's soccer game would cause her to go to bed early? Maybe it wore her out, so we could look for something like "tired" to go in the blank.
3. Look for inaccurate answer choices and eliminate them. If Kaitlin were "thrilled," "competitive," or "inspired" as a result of her soccer game, this wouldn't explain why she had to go to bed early. Therefore, you can eliminate answers (A), (C), and (D).

4. Make an educated guess, or choose the answer you feel most confident about. Since you made a fantastic prediction and used Process of Elimination, you only have one choice left: (B). "Exhausted" is the correct answer—you just earned yourself a point!

HOW CAN YOU MANAGE YOUR STRESS?

If you have ever taken a big test before, or had an important sports match, play, or presentation, then you know what anxiety feels like. Even if you are excited for an approaching event, you might feel nervous. You might begin to doubt yourself, and you might feel as if your mind is racing while butterflies flutter in your stomach!

When it comes to preparing for the ISEE, the good news is that a little anxiety (or adrenaline) goes a long way. Anxiety is a natural, motivating force that will help you study hard in the days leading up to your test. That anxiety will also help you stay alert and work efficiently during the test.

Sometimes, however, anxiety might become larger than life and start to get the best of you. To prevent anxiety and nerves from clouding your ability to work effectively and believe in yourself, you should try some of the suggestions below. Many of these suggestions are good ideas to use in everyday life, but they become especially important in the final week before your test and on test day itself.

- **Relax and slow down.** To center yourself and ease your anxiety, take a big, deep breath. Slowly inhale for a few seconds and then slowly exhale for a few seconds. Shut your eyes and relax. Stretch your arms, roll your neck gently, crack your knuckles—get in the zone of Zen! Continue to breathe deeply and slowly until you can literally feel your body calm down.
- **Picture your goals.** Close your eyes or just pause to reflect on what you want to achieve on test day. Visualize your success, whether that means simply answering all the math questions or getting a top score and gaining acceptance into the school of your dreams. Acknowledge your former successes and abilities, and believe in yourself.
- **Break it down.** Instead of trying to study a whole section at once, break up your studying into small and manageable chunks. Outline your study goals before you start. For example, instead of trying to master the entire Reading Comprehension section at once, you might want to work on one type of passage at a time.
- **Sleep.** Make sure you get plenty of rest and sleep, especially the two nights leading up to your exam!
- **Fuel up.** Eat healthy, filling meals that fuel your brain. Also, drink lots of water to stay hydrated.
- **Take a break.** Put down the books and go play outside, read, listen to music, exercise, or have a good conversation with friend or family member. A good break can be just as restful as a nap. However, watching television will provide minimal relaxation.

On the night before the exam, study only lightly. Make a list of your three biggest fears and work on them, but don't try to learn anything new. Pick out what you are going to wear to the exam—try wearing layers in case the exam room is hotter or colder than you expect. Organize everything you need to bring. Know where the test center is located and how long it will take to get there. Have a nutritious meal and get plenty of sleep!

On the morning of the exam, let your adrenaline kick in naturally. Eat a good breakfast and stay hydrated; your body needs fuel to endure the test. Bring along several pencils and a good eraser. Listen carefully to the test proctor's instructions and let the proctor know if you are left-handed so you can sit at an appropriate desk. Take a deep breath and remember: you are smart and accomplished! Believe in yourself and you will do just fine.

PRACTICE TESTS

CHAPTER 3

PRACTICE TEST 1

MIDDLE LEVEL

HOW TO TAKE THIS PRACTICE TEST

To simulate an accurate testing environment, sit at a desk in a quiet location free of distractions—no TV, computers, phones, music, or noise—and clear your desk of all materials except pencils and erasers. Remember that no calculators, rulers, protractors, dictionaries, or other aids are allowed on the ISEE.

Give yourself the following amounts of time for each section:

SECTION	SUBJECT	TIME LIMIT
1	Verbal Reasoning	20 minutes
2	Quantitative Reasoning	35 minutes
	5 minute break	
3	Reading Comprehension	35 minutes
4	Mathematics Achievement	40 minutes
	5 minute break	
5	Essay	30 minutes

Have an adult help you monitor your time, or use a watch and time yourself. Only give yourself the allotted time for each section; put your pencil down when your time is up.

Follow the instructions carefully. As you take your test, bubble your answers into the answer sheets provided. Use the test booklet as scratch paper for notes and calculations. Remember that you are not granted time at the end of a section to transfer your answers to the answer sheet, so you must do this as you go along.

When you are finished, check your answers against the answer keys provided. Then, score your exam using the directions at the end of the book.

Note: students with diagnosed learning disabilities who apply for testing with accommodations may receive extra time, or may be allowed to use certain assistive devices during the ISEE. For more information, visit http://erblearn.org/parents/admission/isee/accommodations.

Ivy Global

ISEE
MIDDLE LEVEL TEST 1

MARKING INSTRUCTIONS

- Use a #2 or HB pencil only on pages 34 and 35.
- Use a ballpoint pen for your essay on pages 36 and 37.
- Make dark marks that completely fill the circle.
- Erase clearly any mark you wish to change.
- Make no stray marks on this form.
- Do not fold or crease this form.

Correct Mark  Incorrect Marks 

1 VERBAL REASONING

1 Ⓐ Ⓑ Ⓒ Ⓓ	15 Ⓐ Ⓑ Ⓒ Ⓓ	29 Ⓐ Ⓑ Ⓒ Ⓓ
2 Ⓐ Ⓑ Ⓒ Ⓓ	16 Ⓐ Ⓑ Ⓒ Ⓓ	30 Ⓐ Ⓑ Ⓒ Ⓓ
3 Ⓐ Ⓑ Ⓒ Ⓓ	17 Ⓐ Ⓑ Ⓒ Ⓓ	31 Ⓐ Ⓑ Ⓒ Ⓓ
4 Ⓐ Ⓑ Ⓒ Ⓓ	18 Ⓐ Ⓑ Ⓒ Ⓓ	32 Ⓐ Ⓑ Ⓒ Ⓓ
5 Ⓐ Ⓑ Ⓒ Ⓓ	19 Ⓐ Ⓑ Ⓒ Ⓓ	33 Ⓐ Ⓑ Ⓒ Ⓓ
6 Ⓐ Ⓑ Ⓒ Ⓓ	20 Ⓐ Ⓑ Ⓒ Ⓓ	34 Ⓐ Ⓑ Ⓒ Ⓓ Lower Level Ends
7 Ⓐ Ⓑ Ⓒ Ⓓ	21 Ⓐ Ⓑ Ⓒ Ⓓ	35 Ⓐ Ⓑ Ⓒ Ⓓ
8 Ⓐ Ⓑ Ⓒ Ⓓ	22 Ⓐ Ⓑ Ⓒ Ⓓ	36 Ⓐ Ⓑ Ⓒ Ⓓ
9 Ⓐ Ⓑ Ⓒ Ⓓ	23 Ⓐ Ⓑ Ⓒ Ⓓ	37 Ⓐ Ⓑ Ⓒ Ⓓ
10 Ⓐ Ⓑ Ⓒ Ⓓ	24 Ⓐ Ⓑ Ⓒ Ⓓ	38 Ⓐ Ⓑ Ⓒ Ⓓ
11 Ⓐ Ⓑ Ⓒ Ⓓ	25 Ⓐ Ⓑ Ⓒ Ⓓ	39 Ⓐ Ⓑ Ⓒ Ⓓ
12 Ⓐ Ⓑ Ⓒ Ⓓ	26 Ⓐ Ⓑ Ⓒ Ⓓ	40 Ⓐ Ⓑ Ⓒ Ⓓ Middle/Upper Level Ends
13 Ⓐ Ⓑ Ⓒ Ⓓ	27 Ⓐ Ⓑ Ⓒ Ⓓ	
14 Ⓐ Ⓑ Ⓒ Ⓓ	28 Ⓐ Ⓑ Ⓒ Ⓓ	

2 QUANTITATIVE REASONING

1 Ⓐ Ⓑ Ⓒ Ⓓ	15 Ⓐ Ⓑ Ⓒ Ⓓ	29 Ⓐ Ⓑ Ⓒ Ⓓ
2 Ⓐ Ⓑ Ⓒ Ⓓ	16 Ⓐ Ⓑ Ⓒ Ⓓ	30 Ⓐ Ⓑ Ⓒ Ⓓ
3 Ⓐ Ⓑ Ⓒ Ⓓ	17 Ⓐ Ⓑ Ⓒ Ⓓ	31 Ⓐ Ⓑ Ⓒ Ⓓ
4 Ⓐ Ⓑ Ⓒ Ⓓ	18 Ⓐ Ⓑ Ⓒ Ⓓ	32 Ⓐ Ⓑ Ⓒ Ⓓ
5 Ⓐ Ⓑ Ⓒ Ⓓ	19 Ⓐ Ⓑ Ⓒ Ⓓ	33 Ⓐ Ⓑ Ⓒ Ⓓ
6 Ⓐ Ⓑ Ⓒ Ⓓ	20 Ⓐ Ⓑ Ⓒ Ⓓ	34 Ⓐ Ⓑ Ⓒ Ⓓ
7 Ⓐ Ⓑ Ⓒ Ⓓ	21 Ⓐ Ⓑ Ⓒ Ⓓ	35 Ⓐ Ⓑ Ⓒ Ⓓ
8 Ⓐ Ⓑ Ⓒ Ⓓ	22 Ⓐ Ⓑ Ⓒ Ⓓ	36 Ⓐ Ⓑ Ⓒ Ⓓ
9 Ⓐ Ⓑ Ⓒ Ⓓ	23 Ⓐ Ⓑ Ⓒ Ⓓ	37 Ⓐ Ⓑ Ⓒ Ⓓ **Middle/Upper Level Ends**
10 Ⓐ Ⓑ Ⓒ Ⓓ	24 Ⓐ Ⓑ Ⓒ Ⓓ	38 Ⓐ Ⓑ Ⓒ Ⓓ **Lower Level Ends**
11 Ⓐ Ⓑ Ⓒ Ⓓ	25 Ⓐ Ⓑ Ⓒ Ⓓ	
12 Ⓐ Ⓑ Ⓒ Ⓓ	26 Ⓐ Ⓑ Ⓒ Ⓓ	
13 Ⓐ Ⓑ Ⓒ Ⓓ	27 Ⓐ Ⓑ Ⓒ Ⓓ	
14 Ⓐ Ⓑ Ⓒ Ⓓ	28 Ⓐ Ⓑ Ⓒ Ⓓ	

3 READING COMPREHENSION

1 Ⓐ Ⓑ Ⓒ Ⓓ	15 Ⓐ Ⓑ Ⓒ Ⓓ	29 Ⓐ Ⓑ Ⓒ Ⓓ
2 Ⓐ Ⓑ Ⓒ Ⓓ	16 Ⓐ Ⓑ Ⓒ Ⓓ	30 Ⓐ Ⓑ Ⓒ Ⓓ
3 Ⓐ Ⓑ Ⓒ Ⓓ	17 Ⓐ Ⓑ Ⓒ Ⓓ	31 Ⓐ Ⓑ Ⓒ Ⓓ
4 Ⓐ Ⓑ Ⓒ Ⓓ	18 Ⓐ Ⓑ Ⓒ Ⓓ	32 Ⓐ Ⓑ Ⓒ Ⓓ
5 Ⓐ Ⓑ Ⓒ Ⓓ	19 Ⓐ Ⓑ Ⓒ Ⓓ	33 Ⓐ Ⓑ Ⓒ Ⓓ
6 Ⓐ Ⓑ Ⓒ Ⓓ	20 Ⓐ Ⓑ Ⓒ Ⓓ	34 Ⓐ Ⓑ Ⓒ Ⓓ
7 Ⓐ Ⓑ Ⓒ Ⓓ	21 Ⓐ Ⓑ Ⓒ Ⓓ	35 Ⓐ Ⓑ Ⓒ Ⓓ
8 Ⓐ Ⓑ Ⓒ Ⓓ	22 Ⓐ Ⓑ Ⓒ Ⓓ	36 Ⓐ Ⓑ Ⓒ Ⓓ **Middle/Upper Level Ends**
9 Ⓐ Ⓑ Ⓒ Ⓓ	23 Ⓐ Ⓑ Ⓒ Ⓓ	
10 Ⓐ Ⓑ Ⓒ Ⓓ	24 Ⓐ Ⓑ Ⓒ Ⓓ	
11 Ⓐ Ⓑ Ⓒ Ⓓ	25 Ⓐ Ⓑ Ⓒ Ⓓ **Lower Level Ends**	
12 Ⓐ Ⓑ Ⓒ Ⓓ	26 Ⓐ Ⓑ Ⓒ Ⓓ	
13 Ⓐ Ⓑ Ⓒ Ⓓ	27 Ⓐ Ⓑ Ⓒ Ⓓ	
14 Ⓐ Ⓑ Ⓒ Ⓓ	28 Ⓐ Ⓑ Ⓒ Ⓓ	

4 MATHEMATICS ACHIEVEMENT

1 Ⓐ Ⓑ Ⓒ Ⓓ	18 Ⓐ Ⓑ Ⓒ Ⓓ	35 Ⓐ Ⓑ Ⓒ Ⓓ
2 Ⓐ Ⓑ Ⓒ Ⓓ	19 Ⓐ Ⓑ Ⓒ Ⓓ	36 Ⓐ Ⓑ Ⓒ Ⓓ
3 Ⓐ Ⓑ Ⓒ Ⓓ	20 Ⓐ Ⓑ Ⓒ Ⓓ	37 Ⓐ Ⓑ Ⓒ Ⓓ
4 Ⓐ Ⓑ Ⓒ Ⓓ	21 Ⓐ Ⓑ Ⓒ Ⓓ	38 Ⓐ Ⓑ Ⓒ Ⓓ
5 Ⓐ Ⓑ Ⓒ Ⓓ	22 Ⓐ Ⓑ Ⓒ Ⓓ	39 Ⓐ Ⓑ Ⓒ Ⓓ
6 Ⓐ Ⓑ Ⓒ Ⓓ	23 Ⓐ Ⓑ Ⓒ Ⓓ	40 Ⓐ Ⓑ Ⓒ Ⓓ
7 Ⓐ Ⓑ Ⓒ Ⓓ	24 Ⓐ Ⓑ Ⓒ Ⓓ	41 Ⓐ Ⓑ Ⓒ Ⓓ
8 Ⓐ Ⓑ Ⓒ Ⓓ	25 Ⓐ Ⓑ Ⓒ Ⓓ	42 Ⓐ Ⓑ Ⓒ Ⓓ
9 Ⓐ Ⓑ Ⓒ Ⓓ	26 Ⓐ Ⓑ Ⓒ Ⓓ	43 Ⓐ Ⓑ Ⓒ Ⓓ
10 Ⓐ Ⓑ Ⓒ Ⓓ	27 Ⓐ Ⓑ Ⓒ Ⓓ	44 Ⓐ Ⓑ Ⓒ Ⓓ
11 Ⓐ Ⓑ Ⓒ Ⓓ	28 Ⓐ Ⓑ Ⓒ Ⓓ	45 Ⓐ Ⓑ Ⓒ Ⓓ
12 Ⓐ Ⓑ Ⓒ Ⓓ	29 Ⓐ Ⓑ Ⓒ Ⓓ	46 Ⓐ Ⓑ Ⓒ Ⓓ
13 Ⓐ Ⓑ Ⓒ Ⓓ	30 Ⓐ Ⓑ Ⓒ Ⓓ **Lower Level Ends**	47 Ⓐ Ⓑ Ⓒ Ⓓ **Middle/Upper Level Ends**
14 Ⓐ Ⓑ Ⓒ Ⓓ	31 Ⓐ Ⓑ Ⓒ Ⓓ	
15 Ⓐ Ⓑ Ⓒ Ⓓ	32 Ⓐ Ⓑ Ⓒ Ⓓ	
16 Ⓐ Ⓑ Ⓒ Ⓓ	33 Ⓐ Ⓑ Ⓒ Ⓓ	
17 Ⓐ Ⓑ Ⓒ Ⓓ	34 Ⓐ Ⓑ Ⓒ Ⓓ	

STUDENT NAME ______________________ GRADE APPLYING FOR ________

Use a blue or black ballpoint pen to write the final draft of your essay on this sheet.

You must write your essay topic in this space.

Use specific details and examples in your response.

Section 1
Verbal Reasoning

40 Questions | Time: 20 minutes

This section is divided into two parts that contain two different types of questions. As soon as you have completed Part One, answer the questions in Part Two. You may write in your test booklet. For each answer you select, fill in the corresponding circle on your answer document.

PART ONE — SYNONYMS

Each question in Part One consists of a word in capital letters followed by four answer choices. Select the one word that is most nearly the same in meaning as the word in capital letters.

SAMPLE QUESTION:

CHARGE:

(A) release
(B) belittle
(C) accuse
(D) conspire

Sample Answer
Ⓐ Ⓑ ● Ⓓ

The correct answer is "accuse," so circle C is darkened.

PART TWO — SENTENCE COMPLETION

Each question in Part Two is made up of a sentence with one blank. Each blank indicates that a word is missing. The sentence is followed by four answer choices. Select the word that will best complete the meaning of the sentence as a whole.

SAMPLE QUESTIONS:

It rained so much that the streets were -------.

(A) flooded
(B) arid
(C) paved
(D) crowded

Sample Answer
● Ⓑ Ⓒ Ⓓ

The correct answer is "flooded," so circle A is darkened.

STOP. Do not go on until told to do so.

PART TWO — QUANTITATIVE COMPARISONS

All questions in Part Two are quantitative comparisons between the quantities shown in Column A and Column B. Using the information given in each question, compare the quantity in Column A to the quantity in Column B, and choose one of these four answer choices:

(A) The quantity in Column A is greater.
(B) The quantity in Column B is greater.
(C) The two quantities are equal.
(D) The relationship cannot be determined from the information given.

SAMPLE QUESTIONS:

Column A	Column B	Sample Answer
5	$\sqrt{25}$	Ⓐ Ⓑ ● Ⓓ

The quantity in Column A (5) is the same as the quantity in Column B (5), so circle C is darkened.

$x = 6^2 - 3 \times 4$

Column A	Column B	Sample Answer
x	22	● Ⓑ Ⓒ Ⓓ

The quantity in Column A (24) is greater than the quantity in Column B (22), so circle A is darkened.

STOP. Do not go on until told to do so.

STOP

QR

2

PART ONE – WORD PROBLEMS

Directions: Choose the best answer from the four choices given.

1. In the city of Townville, there are C cars, T tricycles, B bicycles, and one high-speed train called the Arrow that runs on sixteen wheels. Which of the following expressions gives the total number of all wheels in Townville?

   (A) $2C + 3T + 2B + 16$

   (B) $4C + 3B + 2T + A$

   (C) $2C + 3T + 2B + A$

   (D) $4C + 3T + 2B + 16$

2. Dan is creating a list of songs in the following pattern: one classical song, one rock song, one country song, one jazz song, one blues song. If this pattern continues, the 48th song in his list will be

   (A) classical

   (B) rock

   (C) country

   (D) jazz

3. If N is a negative number, which of the following expressions has the greatest value?

   (A) $-\frac{N}{2}$

   (B) $N - 2$

   (C) $N - 3$

   (D) N

4. If Q is a positive number, which of the following expressions has the smallest value?

   (A) $-4 - Q$

   (B) $Q - 2$

   (C) $(-Q)^2$

   (D) $-Q$

5. Use the following equations to answer the question.

   $$n = \blacksquare x$$

   $$x = \bigcirc b$$

   What is the value of n if $b = \blacksquare$?

   (A) $\bigcirc$

   (B) $\bigcirc\blacksquare$

   (C) $\blacksquare^2$

   (D) $\bigcirc\blacksquare^2$

6. In the figure below, four line segments are drawn from the midpoints of a large square to make a smaller shaded square. If the area of the large square is $4z$, then what is the area of the shaded square?

   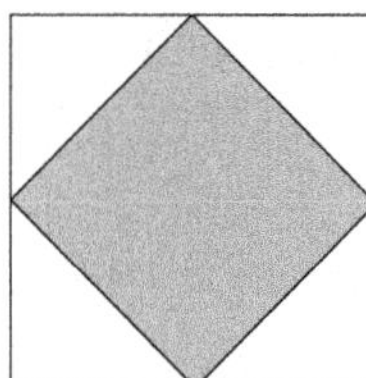

   (A) $\frac{1}{4}z$

   (B) $\frac{1}{3}z$

   (C) z

   (D) $2z$

7. 3 people can pack x boxes in 15 minutes. If they work at the same rate, how many boxes can 6 people pack in 30 minutes?

   (A) $x/2$

   (B) $2x$

   (C) $(2x)^2$

   (D) $4x$

Go on to the next page ➡

8. Ashley has a number of boxes that measure $6 \times 5 \times 10$ inches. She wants to fill the boxes with books that are 5 inches wide, 9 inches tall, and 1.5 inches thick. What is the greatest number of books that Ashley can put in each box?

(A) 2

(B) 3

(C) 4

(D) 5

9. For all real numbers, $\boxed{a} = a^2 + 3^2$.

For example, $\boxed{3} = 3^2 + 3^2 = 9 + 9 = 18$.

What is the value of $\boxed{6}$?

(A) 9

(B) 36

(C) 45

(D) 72

10. Dave and Ryan spent x dollars on a whole pizza. When they ate $^3/_4$ of the pizza, they had 4 slices left over. What was the average cost per slice of pizza?

(A) $\frac{x}{16}$ dollars

(B) $\frac{x}{4}$ dollars

(C) x dollars

(D) $\frac{3x}{16}$ dollars

11. Kathy has replaced all of her incandescent light bulbs with fluorescent light bulbs that last 8 times longer. Compared with how frequently Kathy had to change her incandescent light bulbs previously, how frequently will she now have to change her new light bulbs?

(A) 8% as frequently

(B) 12.5% as frequently

(C) 15% as frequently

(D) 80% as frequently

12. In Figure 3, a cube has a side length of n. How much volume remains if we cut the cube in half diagonally?

Figure 3

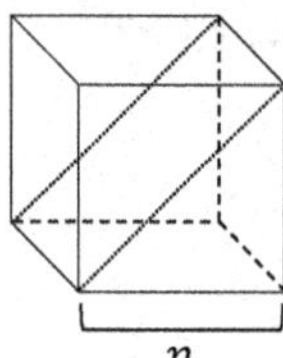

(A) $\frac{n^2}{2}$

(B) $\frac{n^3}{2}$

(C) n^2

(D) n^3

13. If $M = \frac{⍓}{2}$ and $N = 4M$, which expression below is correct?

(A) $N =$ ⍓

(B) $N = 2 \times$ ⍓

(C) $N = 4 \times$ ⍓

(D) $N = M$

14. There are 10 bathtubs each filled to $\frac{1}{3}$ of their capacity with water. Another bathtub is filled to $\frac{2}{3}$ of its capacity with water. If all bathtubs are the same shape and size, how much, on average, are each of the 11 bathtubs filled?

(A) $\frac{1}{3}$ capacity

(B) $\frac{4}{11}$ capacity

(C) $\frac{2}{3}$ capacity

(D) $\frac{11}{15}$ capacity

Go on to the next page ➡

15. A school teacher needs to buy 8 erasers at \$1.10 each. There is a fee of \$5.00 for shipping and an additional tax of 5% calculated after the shipping cost has been added. What is the total cost for the teacher's order?
(A) \$7.91
(B) \$8.80
(C) \$13.80
(D) \$14.49

16. If the cube below is cut all the way through along the dashed lines, how many triangular sections are created?

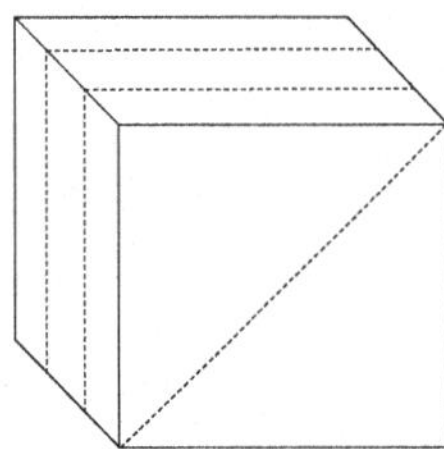

(A) 1
(B) 2
(C) 3
(D) 6

17. Two bedrooms of identical size and dimensions together form the shape of a rectangle. If their total length is l and their total width is w, what is the perimeter of one bedroom?
(A) $\frac{w}{2}+\frac{l}{2}$
(B) $w+l$
(C) $2w+2l$
(D) $2w \times 2l$

18. A number cube has 6 sides numbered 1 through 6. Erol is rolling two number cubes. What is the probability that the sum of his roll will be at least 10?
(A) $\frac{1}{18}$
(B) $\frac{1}{12}$
(C) $\frac{1}{6}$
(D) $\frac{11}{12}$

19. Brynne is digging river-ways for an oncoming flood. Each river-way is 1,000 feet long and is connected to one dam. At each dam, the incoming river-way branches off into three new river-ways. If he begins with one river-way and wants to build a total of 13 river-ways, how many dams does he need?
(A) 3
(B) 4
(C) 13
(D) 39

20. If $a=\frac{b}{c}$ and $d=\left(\frac{c}{b}\right)\div\left(\frac{a}{b}\right)$, which equation is equal to d?
(A) $\frac{1}{b}$
(B) $\frac{c^2}{b}$
(C) 1
(D) $\frac{b}{c}$

Go on to the next page ➡

21. The number of trains leaving Dumbleport Monday through Friday is shown in the chart below.

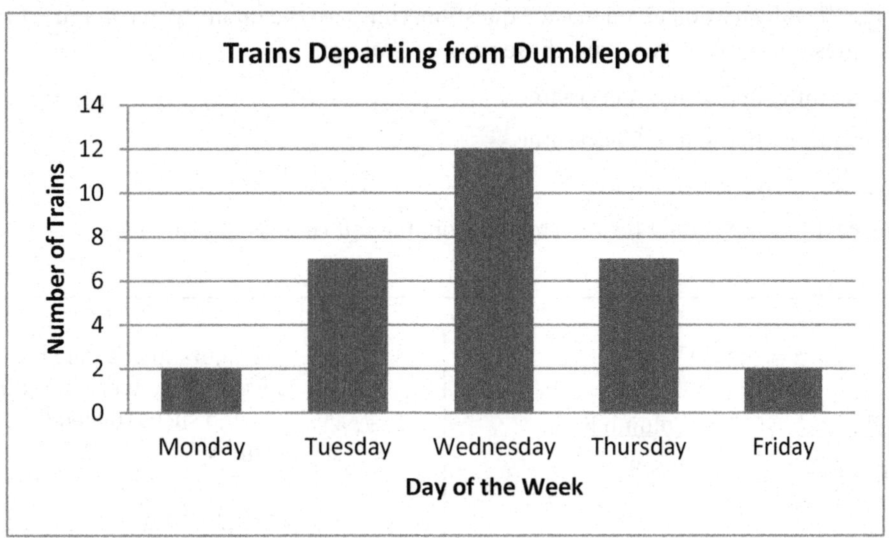

How many fewer trains left from Dumbleport on Friday when compared to the week's average number of daily train departures?

(A) 2

(B) 3

(C) 4

(D) 6

Go on to the next page ➡

PART TWO – QUANTITATIVE COMPARISONS

Directions: Using the information given in each question, compare the quantity in column A to the quantity in Column B. All questions in Part Two have these answer choices:

(A) The quantity in Column A is greater.

(B) The quantity in Column B is greater.

(C) The two quantities are equal.

(D) The relationship cannot be determined from the information given.

$y = -3x + 4$

	Column A	Column B
22.	The value of x when $y = -8$	3

	Column A	Column B
23.	$2^3 - 3^2$	$3^2 - 2^3$

A vase costs $200.00.

	Column A	Column B
24.	A sales tax at 5% of the vase's cost	$15.00

Each person at a party eats four slices of pie. Every pie comes with enough slices to feed exactly three people.

	Column A	Column B
25.	The number of people needed to eat twenty slices of pie	The number of pies needed to feed fifteen people

	Column A	Column B
26.	The slope between (1,2) and (0,3)	The slope of $0.5y = -x + 2$

Paper Route A

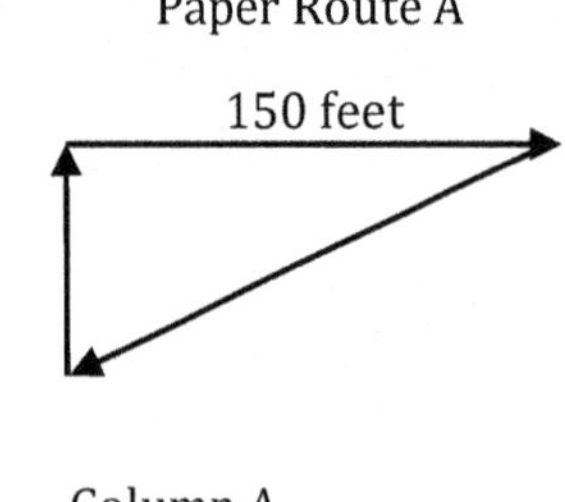

Paper Route B

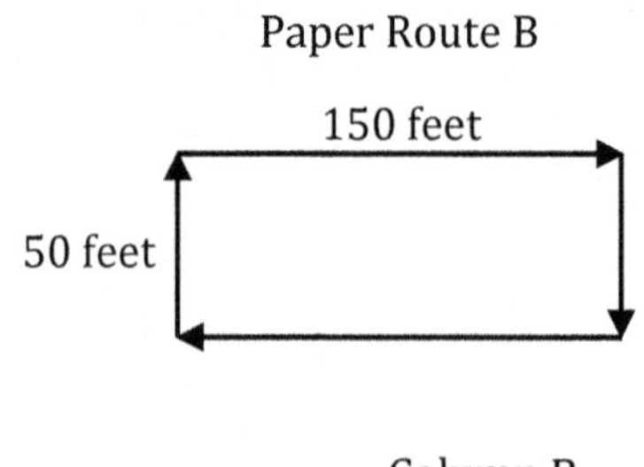

	Column A	Column B
27.	The distance of Paper Route A	The distance of Paper Route B

Go on to the next page ➡

ANSWER CHOICES FOR ALL QUESTIONS ON THIS PAGE:

(A) The quantity in Column A is greater.
(B) The quantity in Column B is greater.
(C) The two quantities are equal.
(D) The relationship cannot be determined from the information given.

A sample is randomly selected from two separate populations. This sample is asked whether they prefer water or milk. The percent of each sample to their respective population and the results of the survey are show in the table below.

City	**A**	**B**
Percent of City Surveyed	20%	40%
People Who Prefer Water	20	30
People Who Prefer Milk	15	30

	Column A	Column B
28.	The predicted number of people who prefer milk in City A	The predicted number of people who prefer milk in City B

Laurel has to get to Chicago from New York. She stops at Allentown, Cleveland, and Toledo along the way to buy sandwiches.

HIGHWAY DISTANCE BETWEEN CITIES	
New York to Allentown	91 miles
Allentown to Cleveland	380 miles
Cleveland to Toledo	116 miles
Toledo to Chicago	246 miles
New York to Allentown	91 miles

	Column A	Column B
29.	The distance remaining on Laurel's trip if she is leaving Cleveland	The distance that Laurel has already traveled if she is leaving Cleveland

Go on to the next page ➡

ANSWER CHOICES FOR ALL QUESTIONS ON THIS PAGE:

(A) The quantity in Column A is greater.
(B) The quantity in Column B is greater.
(C) The two quantities are equal.
(D) The relationship cannot be determined from the information given.

A number cube has six sides numbered 1-6. A deck of cards has 52 cards in total, four of which are king cards.

	Column A	Column B
30.	The probability of rolling a 2 twice in a row with a number cube	The probability of picking one king from a deck of cards

	Column A	Column B
31.	$\frac{\sqrt{25-9}}{\sqrt{36-25}}$	$\frac{(5-3)}{(6-5)}$

A triangle is placed within a square as shown in the diagram below.

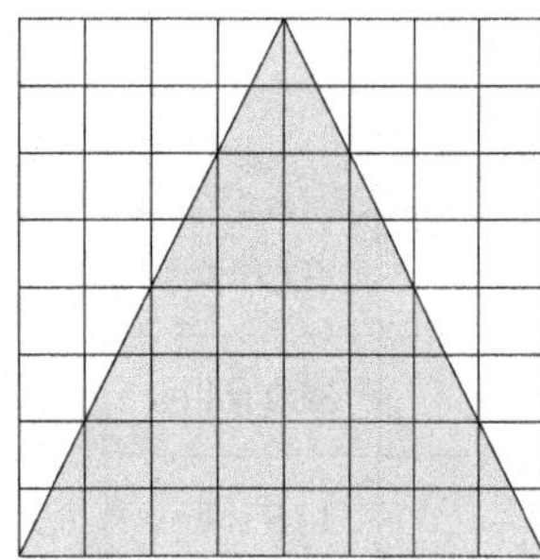

	Column A	Column B
32.	The area of the shaded triangle	The non-shaded area

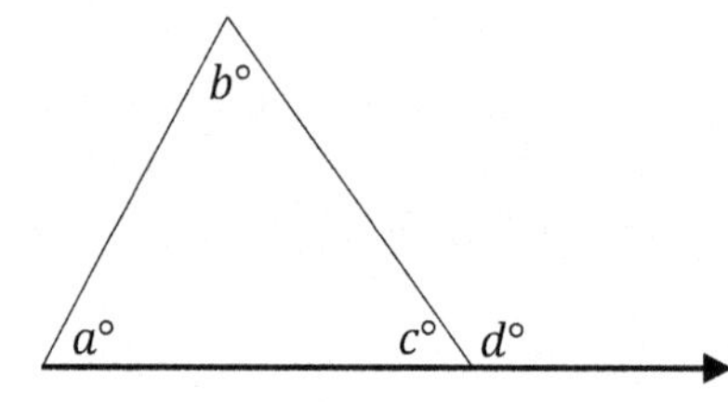

	Column A	Column B
33.	$a+b+c$	$c+d$

$M = \frac{1}{N}$ $\quad N = \frac{1}{L}$

	Column A	Column B
34.	The value of N if $L = \frac{1}{5}$	The value of M if $L = 6$

Eight pool balls are labeled 1-8 and placed in a bag.

	Column A	Column B
35.	The probability of picking a ball labeled with an even number	The probability of picking a ball labeled 6 or greater

Go on to the next page ➡

ANSWER CHOICES FOR ALL QUESTIONS ON THIS PAGE:

(A) The quantity in Column A is greater.
(B) The quantity in Column B is greater.
(C) The two quantities are equal.
(D) The relationship cannot be determined from the information given.

	Column A	Column B
36.	The perimeter of a right angle triangle with one side that measures 5 cm	The perimeter of a right angle triangle with two sides that measure 3 cm and 4 cm

Roland has one pair each of yellow, orange, and blue socks. He also has one pair each of yellow and black pants. Roland randomly selects one pair of socks and one pair of pants.

	Column A	Column B
37.	The probability that Roland will select a pair of yellow or blue socks with black pants	$\frac{1}{3}$

STOP. Do not go on until told to do so.

Section 3
Reading Comprehension

36 Questions | Time: 35 minutes

This section contains six short reading passages. Each passage is followed by six questions based on its content. Answer the questions following each passage on the basis of what is <u>stated</u> or <u>implied</u> in that passage. You may write in your test booklet.

STOP. Do not go on until told to do so.

STOP

Questions 1–6

A green leaf is green because of the presence of a pigment known as chlorophyll, but chlorophyll is not the only pigment in a leaf. Leaves also contain yellow and orange pigments that are present in the leaf throughout its life, and red and purple pigments that develop under certain conditions in the late summer. However, as long as the leaf has plenty of chlorophyll, green will be the dominant color.

Chlorophyll has a vital function: it captures solar rays and utilizes the resulting energy to manufacture the plant's food through a process called photosynthesis, which can also be observed in algae. The simple sugars that are produced during this process from water and carbon dioxide gas are the sole source of the carbohydrates the plant needs for growth and development.

Throughout the spring and summer, the plant continually replenishes the chlorophyll in its leaves so that they can keep producing its food. In late summer, as daylight hours shorten and temperatures cool, the veins that carry fluids into and out of the leaf are gradually closed off as a layer of special cork cells forms at the base of each leaf. As this cork layer develops, the flow of chlorophyll into the leaf decreases, slowly at first, and then rapidly. Eventually, the flow of the replacement chlorophyll cannot keep pace with the rate at which the chlorophyll is used up, and the leaf begins to change colors. Without the chlorophyll there to mask them, the yellow, orange, red, and purple colors of the other leaf pigments begin to show through.

The colors revealed by the absence of chlorophyll can be vibrant and beautiful, though they only last for a few weeks in the fall. Certain areas, like southern Canada and the eastern United States, are even internationally famous for the brilliance of their "fall foliage." These areas and others often attract tourists called "leaf peepers" who travel great distances for a chance to see the changing leaves.

Go on to the next page ➡

1. According to the passage, a leaf's supply of chlorophyll is replenished by
   (A) the formation of cork cells at the base of each leaf.
   (B) water condensation from the atmosphere.
   (C) veins that transport fluids into each leaf.
   (D) the production of carbohydrates.

2. As it is used in line 11, "vital" most nearly means
   (A) critical.
   (B) energetic.
   (C) active.
   (D) refreshing.

3. Red, yellow, and purple leaf pigments reveal themselves
   (A) during the process of photosynthesis.
   (B) when a leaf has less chlorophyll.
   (C) on cloudy days.
   (D) when a leaf has more chlorophyll.

4. Which question could be answered by information given in the passage?
   (A) What causes the seasons to change?
   (B) Why are leaves green, and why do they change color?
   (C) Why are some trees always green?
   (D) Why do plant leaves contain yellow and orange pigments?

5. The function of the second paragraph (lines 11–19) is to
   (A) explain why leaves are green.
   (B) provide evidence that contradicts the first paragraph.
   (C) describe the role of chlorophyll in plants.
   (D) summarize the main idea of the passage.

6. It can be inferred from the passage that the more chlorophyll a leaf has
   (A) the greener it will be.
   (B) the less green it will be.
   (C) the less food it can produce.
   (D) the colder it will be.

Go on to the next page ➡

Questions 7–12

Nicknamed the "City of Angels," Los Angeles is a global city, known for its strengths in business, entertainment, media, technology, and sports. The city is home to renowned cultural institutions like the Hollywood Bowl and Getty Center, and is one of the most substantial economies within the United States.

But this paradise is not without its problems: owing to its geography, and heavy traffic, Los Angeles suffers from debilitating air pollution in the form of smog. The Los Angeles Basin is susceptible to atmospheric inversion, meaning the air closest to the earth's surface is colder than the air above. This phenomenon traps the cooler air and the exhaust from road vehicles, airplanes, and other sources close to the ground. Further, unlike other large cities that rely on rain to clear smog, Los Angeles gets only 15 inches of rain each year, allowing pollution to accumulate over many consecutive days. These factors make smog a pressing issue for the city, and the 2006 and 2007 annual reports of the American Lung Association ranked the city as the most polluted in the country.

To tackle this issue, Los Angeles decided to take a legal approach. In 2008 a law was passed allowing the city to collect fees from those using its port for shipping, with the funds raised directed to local air quality projects. The state of California also updated its emission standards in 2012, making them the strictest in the country. As a result, the number of severe smog alerts in Los Angeles has declined from over 100 per year in the 1970s to almost zero in recent years. Smog is expected to continue to drop in the coming years due to new technologies like electric and hybrid cars.

Despite these improvements, much work remains to be done. Indeed, in 2013 Los Angeles was still ranked as having the nation's worst smog. One opportunity that the city should consider is working to improve its public transit system. While Los Angeles already has an extensive bus network, which is the second busiest in the country, only about 10% of the city's residents make use of it. By contrast, other large American cities sometimes see a quarter or more of their inhabitants opting for buses, subways, and trains; in recent years over 50% of New York City residents used such methods to travel to work. Encouraging more citizens to utilize public transportation rather than taking their own cars could be the final piece of the pollution puzzle that gives Los Angeles the cleaner air it craves.

Go on to the next page ➡

7. The main purpose of this passage is to
   (A) describe the history of innovation in Los Angeles.
   (B) explain the concept of atmospheric inversion.
   (C) discuss the problem of smog in Los Angeles and some possible solutions.
   (D) argue for better public transit in Los Angeles.

8. Which best describes the way the passage is organized?
   (A) A series of contradictory solutions are presented.
   (B) A problem and early solutions are described, and a further proposal is discussed.
   (C) A popular view is presented and then challenged by scientific evidence.
   (D) A problem is introduced and then analyzed.

9. In line 21, "pressing" most nearly means
   (A) serious.
   (B) forceful.
   (C) chronic.
   (D) constricted.

10. The author is most likely to agree with which one of the following statements?
   (A) The measures Los Angeles has already taken to limit smog have been helpful but insufficient.
   (B) So far Los Angeles has done nothing to fight smog.
   (C) Even without further action, the current levels of smog in Los Angeles are acceptable.
   (D) Improving public transit is the only way to further reduce smog in Los Angeles.

11. According to the passage, besides geography, the largest cause of smog and pollution in Los Angeles is
   (A) industry.
   (B) entertainment.
   (C) climate.
   (D) transportation.

12. It can be inferred from the passage that electric and hybrid cars
   (A) produce more pollution than traditional cars.
   (B) cannot be used in the Los Angeles basin.
   (C) will encourage more citizens to utilize public transportation.
   (D) produce less pollution than traditional cars.

Go on to the next page ➡

Questions 13–18

To buy a horse was my greatest ambition. My father died; and as misfortunes seldom come singly, the horse on which my family depended to till our scanty fields died shortly after its owner. Whenever the spring arrived, our one chance to plant a crop was to hire a mule from our nearest neighbor, the tanner. I was the eldest son, and my mother had only my work to offer in payment. The tanner always greeted this proposition coldly. The mule was needed to haul up piles of bark from the depths of the woods to the tanyard. Then, too, he had his own crops to plant. Although the mule was a multifarious animal that ploughed and worked in the bark-mill, and hauled bark from the woods, and took long journeys with the wagon or under the saddle, it was impossible for her to be in all the places in which she was urgently needed at the same time. Therefore, to hire her out hardly seemed to benefit her master. Nevertheless, this bargain was struck every spring. My poverty-stricken mother always congratulated herself upon it, and it never occurred to her that the amount of work that I did in the tanyard was more than enough payment for the few days that the tanner's mule ploughed our little fields.

I, however, was beginning to see that a boy to drive that mule around the bark-mill was as essential as the mule himself. As Providence had failed to furnish the tanner with a son for this purpose—his family consisting of several small daughters—I supplied a long-felt want.

I appreciated that my mother was overreached, yet I could not see that she could do otherwise. I sighed for independence, for a larger opportunity. As I drove the mule round the limited circuit, my mind was far away. I anxiously canvassed the future. I cherished fiery, ambitious schemes—but always with a sense of their futility. With my time thus mortgaged, I thought that my help to my mother was far less than it might be. But until I could have a horse of my own, there was no hope—no progress. And for this I planned, and dreamed, and saved.

Go on to the next page ➡

13. When did the family's horse die?
    (A) in the spring.
    (B) before the father died.
    (C) after the father died.
    (D) while it was plowing the field.

14. What deal was struck every spring?
    (A) The tanner gave the narrator's family some bark, and the narrator's mother lent him their horse.
    (B) The narrator drove the tanner's wagon, and the tanner helped the narrator's mother in the field.
    (C) The narrator gave the tanner his crops, and the tanner gave the narrator a horse.
    (D) The tanner lent the narrator's mother his mule, and the narrator did work for the tanner.

15. What is the most likely reason that the narrator's family always struck this deal in the spring?
    (A) The spring was the time of the year when they needed to till their fields to plant a crop.
    (B) Their old horse died in the spring.
    (C) The spring was the time of the year when the tanner didn't need to use the mule.
    (D) It was too cold to walk to the tanner's house during any other time of the year.

16. The passage answers all of the following questions EXCEPT which one?
    (A) Did the narrator have an older brother?
    (B) What did the narrator's family need the mule for?
    (C) What did the narrator want more than anything?
    (D) How many siblings did the narrator have?

17. In line 31, the word "furnish" most nearly means
    (A) provide.
    (B) appoint.
    (C) include.
    (D) trade.

18. Which phrase means most nearly the same as "this bargain was struck" (lines 21-22)?
    (A) this deal was made.
    (B) we hit upon an idea.
    (C) the bargain was rejected.
    (D) we were astonished at the bargain.

Go on to the next page ➡

Questions 19–24

Proudly raising four fingers—representing the four stripes of the Catalan flag—the enxaneta is greeted by uproarious applause, which he or she can usually enjoy only for a moment before scrambling down the other side of the human tower known as a castell.

"Castell" is the Catalan word for, as an English-speaker might guess, "castle." Castells are a Catalan tradition dating back to the 18th century, when they were first built during local festivals in the city of Valls. Today, castell teams—or colles—build elaborate human towers during festivals throughout Catalonia, as well as in competition.

While castell teams were traditionally all-male, today's colles are as diverse as the communities they come from, uniting men and women of all ages in a feat that is bigger than themselves. Each level of the castell is formed by two to five people standing on the shoulders of those in the level below. The enxaneta is the brave soul, almost always a child, who climbs to the top of a castell to mark its completion. Then begins the treacherous process of dismantling the many levels (as many as ten) of castellers who make up the tower. This is the most treacherous stage of the activity, when participants are most likely to fall. But the danger is not quite as great as it might seem—hundreds of supporters form a pinya, or base, for the castell, cushioning the fall of the castellers in case of collapse. In a demonstration of the sportsmanship found among castellers, when not competing, even members of rival colles will assist in forming a pinya for another team that is attempting to build a particularly difficult structure.

The traditional outfit for castellers usually consists of a pair of white trousers and a colorful shirt, often bearing the crest or emblem of the casteller's team. The castellers generally do not wear protective equipment, with the exception of a sash, which provides support for the lower back. Indeed, castellers typically do not even wear shoes, which could injure the people on the lower levels of the Castell, and can actually make it harder to balance.

Go on to the next page ➡

19. Which of the following statements would the author most likely NOT agree with?
    (A) The completion of a castell is an exciting moment for the audience.
    (B) Today's castell teams are better than those of the 18th century.
    (C) Building a castell is an impressive achievement.
    (D) Castellers are actually safer than their audience might imagine.

20. Which best expresses the main point of the passage?
    (A) Building castells started in the 18th century all over Catalonia as an activity that brought men and women together.
    (B) Castells were first built by all-male teams in 18th century Valls; today, men, women, and children build them together all over Catalonia.
    (C) Castells were once popular throughout Catalonia but today are mainly built by the inhabitants of Valls.
    (D) Building castells is a new sport that was designed to heal social rifts by uniting diverse groups in pursuit of a common goal.

21. The attitude of the author towards castells is best described as
    (A) alarmed.
    (B) critical.
    (C) disbelieving.
    (D) admiring.

22. According to the passage, what is the role of the pinya (lines 29-33)?
    (A) The pinya is a crowd of fans that will cheer the castellers even if they fail.
    (B) If the castellers lose their balance and fall, the supporters in the pinya will help them back onto their feet.
    (C) If the castellers lose their balance and fall, they will fall safely onto the pinya instead of hitting the ground.
    (D) The pinya is the child who goes to the top of the castell to signal its completion.

23. Which best describes the organization of the passage?
    (A) A specific event is introduced, and then its history and process are described.
    (B) A hypothesis is presented and arguments to support it are provided.
    (C) A specific event is introduced and then criticized.
    (D) An opinion is presented, followed by facts to support that opinion.

24. In line 13, the word "elaborate" most nearly means
    (A) complex.
    (B) frilly.
    (C) modest.
    (D) compact.

Go on to the next page ➡

Questions 25-30

The following is an excerpt from a speech by Lyndon B. Johnson, delivered in 1964.

A third place to build the Great Society is in the classrooms of America. There your children's lives will be shaped. Our society will not be great until every young mind is set free to scan the farthest reaches of thought and imagination. We are still far from that goal. Today, 8 million adult Americans, more than the entire population of Michigan, have not finished 5 years of school. Nearly 20 million have not finished 8 years of school. Nearly 54 million -- more than one quarter of all America -- have not even finished high school.

Each year more than 100,000 high school graduates, with proved ability, do not enter college because they cannot afford it. And if we cannot educate today's youth, what will we do in 1970 when elementary school enrollment will be 5 million greater than 1960?

In many places, classrooms are overcrowded and curricula are outdated. Most of our qualified teachers are underpaid, and many of our paid teachers are unqualified. So we must give every child a place to sit and a teacher to learn from. Poverty must not be a bar to learning, and learning must offer an escape from poverty.

But more classrooms and more teachers are not enough. We must seek an educational system which grows in excellence as it grows in size. This means better training for our teachers. It means preparing youth to enjoy their hours of leisure as well as their hours of labor. It means exploring new techniques of teaching, to find new ways to stimulate the love of learning and the capacity for creation.

Go on to the next page ➡

25. The passage above mainly focuses on
    (A) arguing for improvements in the educational system.
    (B) outlining the problems with education.
    (C) encouraging more people to stay in school and further their education.
    (D) addressing the issues of poverty by subsidizing education.

26. Which word best describes the speaker's tone when describing steps that should be taken to improve the system of education?
    (A) ambivalent
    (B) petulant
    (C) discouraged
    (D) emphatic

27. The second paragraph (lines 13-18) suggests that the speaker believes that
    (A) the cost of college helps to limit demand to just those students who will benefit the most.
    (B) college education should be made more affordable to capable students.
    (C) every citizen should be given a free college education.
    (D) college is expensive mainly because there are too many capable students.

28. When the speaker says that "we must give every child a place to sit" (line 23), he is making reference to
    (A) the large number of adults who have not graduated from high school.
    (B) the problem of overcrowded classrooms.
    (C) the outdated curricula still being used in schools.
    (D) the lack of schools in rural areas.

29. The passage suggests that a high quality education will help some students
    (A) grow up to escape the poverty of their childhood.
    (B) afford the cost of college tuition.
    (C) spend more of their time on leisure.
    (D) spend more of their time at work.

30. What best describes the speaker's tone when discussing the current state of the education system?
    (A) supportive
    (B) disinterested
    (C) neutral
    (D) critical

Go on to the next page ➡

Questions 31–36

Carrots contain vitamin A. A lack of vitamin A can cause poor vision, including poor night vision. In cases where poor vision is the result of a vitamin deficiency, vision can be restored by adding the vitamin back into the diet. One way to do this is by eating plenty of carrots. Some people, however, believe that the relationship between carrots and vision goes even further, arguing that eating large quantities of carrots will improve vision beyond normal limits and allow one to see in the dark.

This misconception developed in part from stories of British gunners in World War II, who were able to shoot down German planes in the darkness of night. The British gunners were able to shoot down German planes thanks to advances in radar technology, which used radio waves to detect metallic objects like the German planes and accurately target them even in the dark. But the British Government circulated a rumor that it was a diet which included unusually large amounts of carrots that enabled their pilots to see German planes in the dark. This propaganda helped to conceal the recent advances in technology from the Germans by providing a plausible alternative explanation for the success of British gunners. Since German folktales already included such stories about carrots, the story was quite believable to the Germans.

This propaganda also helped to achieve another important goal for the British by increasing British carrot consumption. During the war, ships importing food to Brittan were often sunk, and there were constant shortages of essential foodstuffs – but there was actually a surplus of carrots. By increasing demand for the vegetable with creative stories about its health benefits, the British government was able to encourage the population to consume more of it, thereby relieving strain on the rest of the food supply. Propaganda about carrots also played a role in the "Dig for Victory" campaign, which was designed to encourage Britons to plant gardens and grow their own food locally. The campaign was widely successful, and carrots became an important part of British gardens.

Go on to the next page ➡

31. It can be inferred from the passage that
    (A) British propaganda was more effective against the British than the Germans.
    (B) many Britons planted gardens during the war.
    (C) carrots actually aren't a healthy food after all.
    (D) animals that have good night vision eat a lot of carrots

32. According to the passage, what role did the British Air Force play in the belief that carrots can provide the ability to see in the dark?
    (A) The British Air Force intentionally spread this rumor to misinform the Germans.
    (B) The British Air Force tried to stop this rumor from reaching the Germans.
    (C) The British Air Force told this rumor to their pilots in order to justify the carrots in their rations.
    (D) When the British Air Force heard this rumor, they encouraged their pilots to eat carrots.

33. According to the passage, the British gunners were actually able to shoot down German planes at night because
    (A) the British ate carrots to improve their night vision.
    (B) the light emitted by the German planes made them easy to see.
    (C) the British had naturally better eyesight than the Germans.
    (D) the British used radar technology to find the planes.

34. The main purpose of this passage is to
    (A) give evidence of how carrots can help you see in the dark.
    (B) document German folk stories about carrots.
    (C) discuss the historical importance of carrots in Britain during World War II.
    (D) provide an explanation of World War II-era radar technology.

35. In line 13, the word "misconception" most nearly means
    (A) belief.
    (B) vicious rumor.
    (C) propaganda.
    (D) faulty idea.

36. The passage suggests that propaganda
    (A) had no effect on World War II.
    (B) played an important role in accomplishing certain goals for the British.
    (C) deceived many people and promoted ill will.
    (D) reduced the consumption of carrots in Great Britain.

STOP. Do not go on until told to do so.

STOP

SECTION 4
Mathematics Achievement

47 Questions | **Time: 40 minutes**

Each question is followed by four suggested answers. Read each question and then decide which one of the four suggested answers is best.

Find the row of spaces on your answer document that has the same number as the question. In this row, mark the space having the same letter as the answer you have chosen. You may write in your test booklet.

SAMPLE QUESTION:

Sample Answer

Ⓐ ● Ⓒ Ⓓ

If $a = 3$, what is the value $a^2 + (3 \times 4) \div 6$?

(A) 3.5

(B) 11

(C) 14.5

(D) 20

The correct answer is 11, so circle B is darkened.

STOP. Do not go on until told to do so.

STOP

1. If $Q<2$ and $Q>-1$, which of the following could be a value of Q?

   (A) -1
   (B) 0
   (C) 2
   (D) 2.5

2. If the ratio of $5:12$ is the same as $X:144$, then $X =$

   (A) 25
   (B) 50
   (C) 55
   (D) 60

3. Joe bought a bag of 42 candies. He first gave $^1/_3$ of the bag to his brother, and he then gave 10 pieces of candy to his sister. How many pieces of candy did Joe have remaining?

   (A) 4
   (B) 18
   (C) 10
   (D) 52

4. Figure *AB* is made from pieces *A* and *B*.

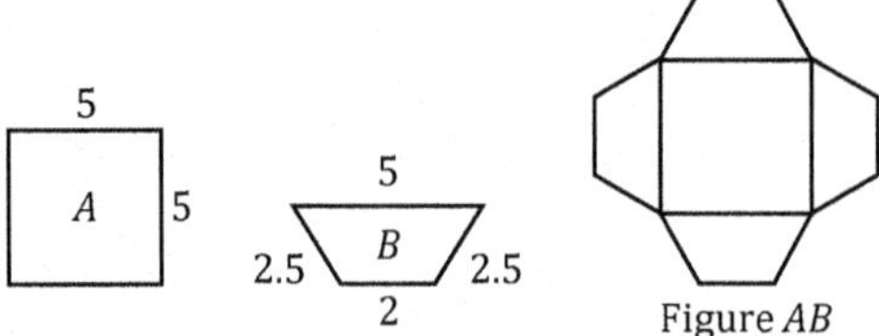

   If *A* is a square and *B* is a trapezoid, what is the perimeter of Figure *AB*?

   (A) 20
   (B) 26
   (C) 28
   (D) 32

5. If the area of a square is 1 cm^2, what is the perimeter of the square?

   (A) 1 cm
   (B) 2 cm
   (C) 3 cm
   (D) 4 cm

6. Mike's soccer team has won 4 games and lost 7 games. There are 11 more games left in the season. How many more games must Mike's team win in order to have an equal number of wins and losses for the whole season?

   (A) 4
   (B) 7
   (C) 9
   (D) 10

7. What is the value of the expression $\frac{5^2-1}{12}$?

   (A) $^1/_3$
   (B) $^1/_2$
   (C) 1
   (D) 2

8. Which of the following is closest to 0.32×59?

   (A) $^1/_6$ of 50
   (B) $^1/_3$ of 50
   (C) $^1/_2$ of 50
   (D) $^1/_3$ of 60

Go on to the next page ➡

9. The figure below shows two squares, one with a side length of 4 and one with a side length of 7.

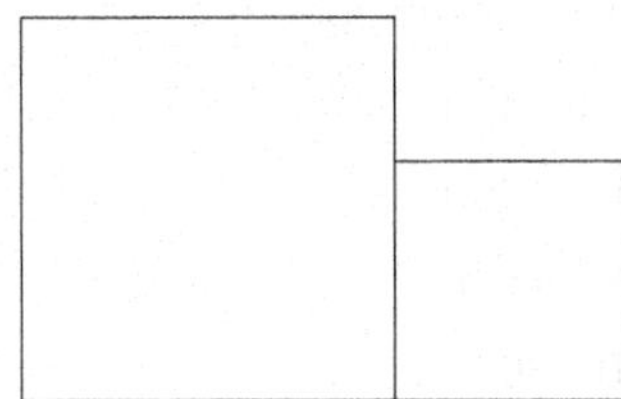

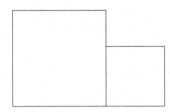

What is the perimeter of the entire figure?

(A) 16

(B) 20

(C) 33

(D) 36

10. A group of 3 knitters takes 3 hours to knit a total of 6 sweaters. Michelle can knit 6 sweaters in 3 hours working by herself. If Michelle joins the group of knitters, what will be the new average rate for each knitter?

(A) $^1/_2$ sweaters per hour

(B) $^2/_3$ sweaters per hour

(C) 1 sweater per hour

(D) $^4/_3$ sweaters per hour

11. There are 230 foxes in a forest. If the ratio of rabbits to foxes in the forest is 5:2, how many rabbits are in the forest?

(A) 460

(B) 575

(C) 720

(D) 1150

Questions 12-13 refer to the chart below:

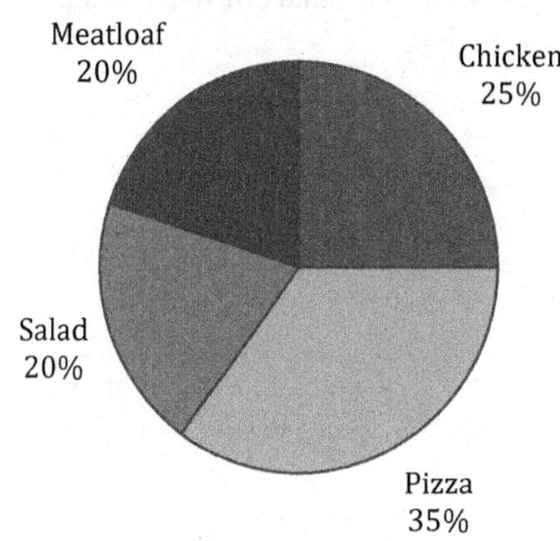

12. The chart above shows the breakdown of students' lunch orders at a cafeteria. If 120 lunches were ordered, how many students ordered pizza?

(A) 28

(B) 35

(C) 36

(D) 42

13. What fraction of students ordered meatloaf or salad?

(A) $^1/_5$

(B) $^2/_5$

(C) $^1/_4$

(D) $^1/_2$

Go on to the next page ➡

14. In the figure below, a square with a side length of 8 is adjacent to a triangle with a base of 8.

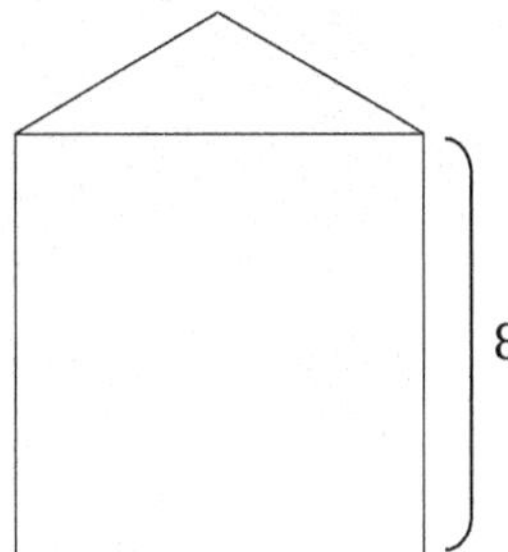

If the height of the entire figure is 10, what is its area?

(A) 56
(B) 64
(C) 72
(D) 80

15. A swimming pool is being filled with water at a rate of 120 cubic feet per hour. If the pool measures 10 feet long by 12 feet wide by 8 feet deep, how long will it take for the pool to be entirely full?

(A) 8 hrs
(B) 12 hrs
(C) 16 hrs
(D) 80 hrs

16. According to the chart below, Author A wrote approximately how many more books than Author E?

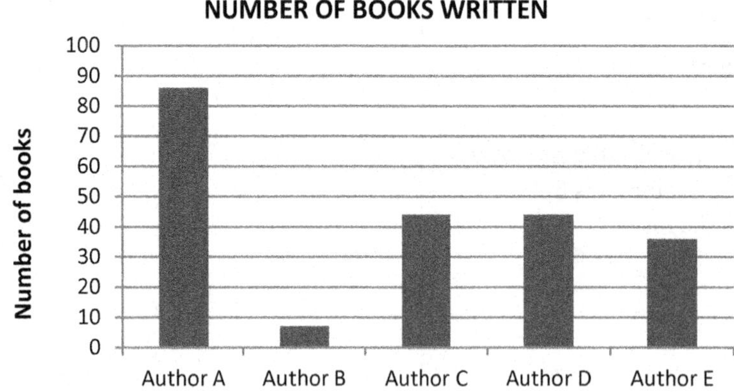

(A) 40
(B) 50
(C) 60
(D) 70

Go on to the next page ➡

17. According to the chart below, what were the approximate average earnings of the three highest-grossing films during the weekend of July 13-15?

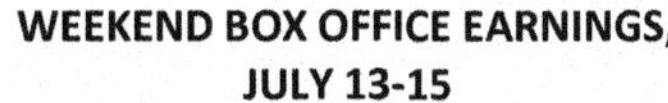

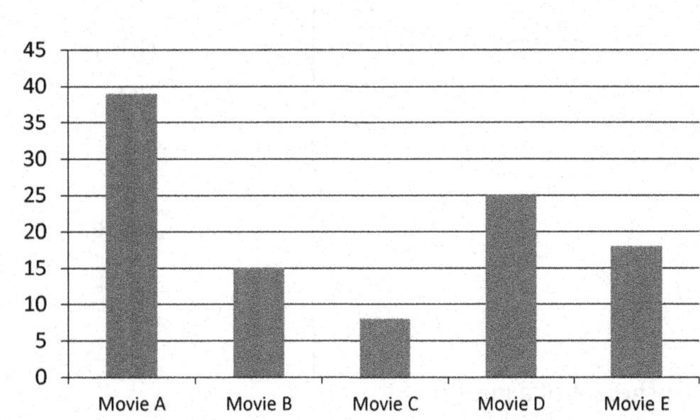

(A) \$20 million
(B) \$30 million
(C) \$40 million
(D) \$50 million

---

18. According to the graph below, pencils were produced at the greatest rate between which years?

PENCILS PRODUCED IN PAST 20 YEARS

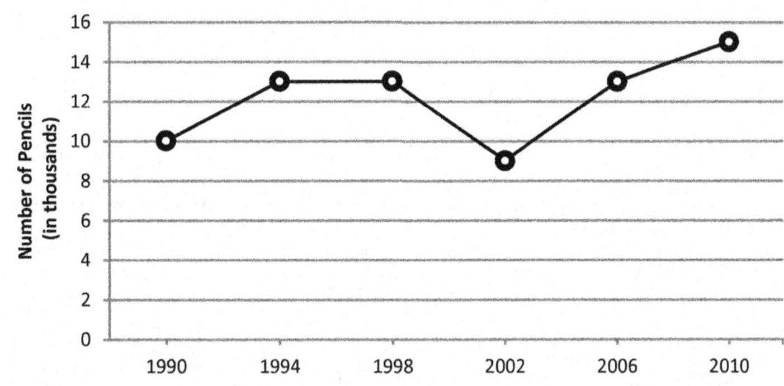

(A) 1994-1998
(B) 1998-2002
(C) 2002-2006
(D) 2006-2010

Go on to the next page ➡

19. Which is equivalent to the following equation?

$$\frac{1}{x} \times \frac{1}{2} + \frac{1}{16} = y$$

(A) $x = \frac{1}{2y - \frac{1}{8}}$

(B) $x = y \times 2 - \frac{1}{16}$

(C) $x = y - \frac{1}{8}$

(D) $x = \left(y - \frac{1}{16}\right) \times 2$

20. If one fourth of the height of a giraffe is 5 ft, what is three fifths of the giraffe's height?

(A) 5 ft

(B) 8 ft

(C) 10 ft

(D) 12 ft

21. A T-shirt is on sale for 25% off of the regular price of $15.99. About how much less in dollars is the sale price?

(A) $3

(B) $4

(C) $8

(D) $12

22. If $\frac{2}{3} + M < \frac{1}{6}$, which of the following could be a value for M?

(A) $-\frac{2}{3}$

(B) $-\frac{1}{2}$

(C) $-\frac{1}{3}$

(D) $\frac{1}{3}$

23. The sum of three consecutive integers is 27. What is the smallest of the three integers?

(A) 8

(B) 9

(C) 10

(D) 11

24. If ★ × 5 = ◆ × 2 and ◆ = 3, what is the value of ★?

(A) $\frac{2}{5}$

(B) $\frac{4}{5}$

(C) $\frac{6}{5}$

(D) 6

25. Gabrielle has packed 11 pieces of clothing for a vacation, including 5 scarves, 3 hats, and 3 pairs of gloves. If she wants to select an outfit that has one scarf, one hat, and one pair of gloves, how many choices does she have?

(A) 3

(B) 11

(C) 45

(D) 60

26. For two numbers p and s, $p \times 2 = s + 2$.

Which expression represents the value of $p \times 3$?

(A) $3 \times s$

(B) $\frac{3}{2} \times s + 3$

(C) $3 \times s + 3$

(D) $s + 6$

27. What is the closest value to $\sqrt{139}$?

(A) 11

(B) 12

(C) 13

(D) 20

Go on to the next page ➡

28. What is the difference between 5621−9586?

(A) -4035

(B) -3965

(C) -3935

(D) -3035

29. Ashley has 10 more pencils than Troy. If Troy has 5 pencils, what fraction of the total pencils does Troy have?

(A) $\frac{1}{2}$

(B) $\frac{1}{3}$

(C) $\frac{1}{4}$

(D) $\frac{1}{5}$

30. Sophia has written 8 novels during her 24-year career. If she continues to write the same average number of novels per year, how many total novels will she have written after another 10 years?

(A) 8

(B) 9

(C) 10

(D) 11

31. 20% of a is equal to b. What is 35% of b, in terms of a?

(A) $0.07a$

(B) $0.14a$

(C) $0.15a$

(D) $0.35a$

32. If $x = \frac{2}{3}y$ and $z = \frac{1}{2}y$, z is equal to

(A) $\frac{x}{4}$

(B) $\frac{3x}{4}$

(C) x

(D) $\frac{4x}{3}$

33. Jared is rolling two six-sided number cubes, numbered 1-6. What is the probability that the sum of his rolls will equal 4?

(A) $\frac{1}{36}$

(B) $\frac{1}{18}$

(C) $\frac{1}{12}$

(D) $\frac{1}{9}$

34. Gerome's weekly wage in dollars (W) relates to the number of hours he works (H) according to the equation below:

$$W = H \times \$7 + \$40$$

What does this formula indicate?

(A) For every 7 hours of work, Gerome makes $47.

(B) When Gerome works 0 hours, his wage is $40.

(C) Gerome pays $40 to begin his work.

(D) Gerome works 47 hours per week.

35. The distance from Buxton to Elmswood is 15 miles. In order to get to Elmswood from Buxton, Sam has to pass through Milton. The distance from Buxton to Milton is 5 miles. What is the approximate distance from Milton to Elmswood, in kilometers? (Note: 1 mile ≈ 1.6 kilometers)

(A) 10 kilometers

(B) 16 kilometers

(C) 24 kilometers

(D) 5 kilometers

Go on to the next page ➡

36. What coordinate pair would complete a rhombus on the coordinate plane below?

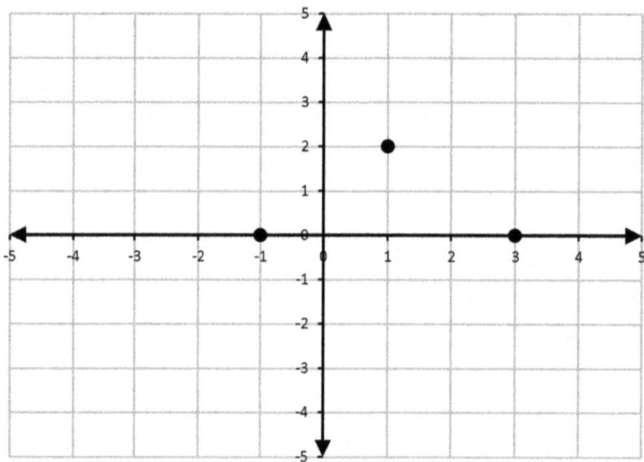

(A) $(-2,1)$
(B) $(1,-2)$
(C) $(0,0)$
(D) $(1,2)$

---

37. In the coordinate plane below, if ΔABC were reflected along the y axis, what would be the new coordinates for point C?

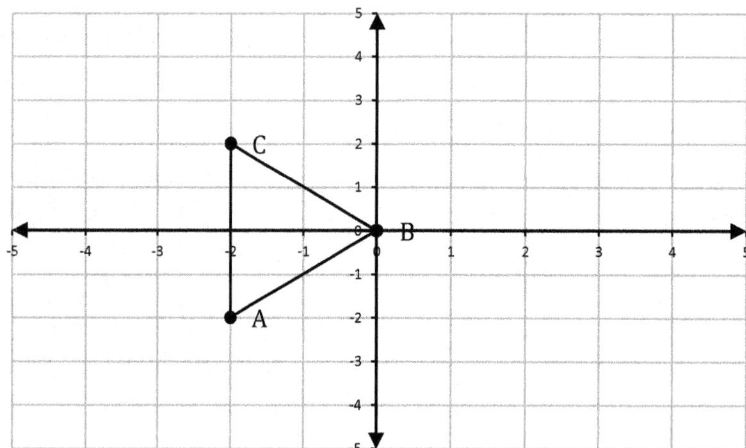

(A) $(-2,-2)$
(B) $(-2,2)$
(C) $(2,-2)$
(D) $(2,2)$

Go on to the next page ➡

38. Two spinners are each equally divided into three parts with the colors red, green, and yellow. If Stacy spins both spinners, what is the probability that each spinner will land on red or green?

(A) $\frac{2}{9}$

(B) $\frac{4}{9}$

(C) $\frac{4}{6}$

(D) $\frac{5}{6}$

39. Which expression is equal to 144?

(A) $3 + 1 \times 3 \times (4 \times 4 - 1)$

(B) $(3 + 1) \times (3 \times 4) \times 4 - 1$

(C) $3 + (1 \times 3) \times (4 \times 4) - 1$

(D) $(3 + 1) \times 3 \times 4 \times (4 - 1)$

40. If $P = 2 \times (\pi \times r)$, what is P when $r =$ 6.28 inches?

(A) 6.253 π inches

(B) 8 π inches

(C) 12.56 π inches

(D) 25.12 π inches

41. What is the greatest common prime factor of 42 and 63?

(A) 3

(B) 7

(C) 9

(D) 11

42. Continue the pattern:

(A) 

(B) 

(C) 

(D) 

Go on to the next page ➡

43. What is the closest estimate of $(63 \times 98) \div 5032$?

(A) 0.1

(B) 1.2

(C) 1.5

(D) 2.0

44. If $z = \frac{3}{4}y$ and $y = 1.2$, then which expression best represents the value of $2z$?

(A) $\frac{21}{20}$

(B) $\frac{3}{2}$

(C) $\frac{24}{15}$

(D) $\frac{9}{5}$

45. One candy bar costs $0.89, an orange costs $1.21, and a pair of tweezers costs $2.12. If Ho-jung has a $5.00 bill, how much change will he receive if he purchases a candy bar, an orange and one pair of tweezers?

(A) $0.69

(B) $0.78

(C) $2.33

(D) $3.20

46. If $\frac{3}{6x} = 21$, what is the value of $\frac{1}{3x}$?

(A) 14

(B) 18

(C) 21

(D) 36

47. The Opera Company of New York is planning its production run of the Magic Flute. The cost to pay its cast and crew is $2,401.51. The opera hall seats 200 people, tickets are $24.98 each, and the performance is sold out. What is the expected profit for the show after paying its cast and crew?

(A) $2,534.49

(B) $2,535.49

(C) $2,594.49

(D) $4,996.00

STOP. Do not go on until told to do so.

STOP

Essay Topic Sheet

The directions for the Essay portion of the ISEE are printed in the box below. Use the pre-lined pages on pages 36-37 for this part of the Practice Test.

You will have 30 minutes to plan and write an essay on the topic printed on the other side of this page. **Do not write on another topic. An essay on another topic is not acceptable.**

The essay is designed to give you an opportunity to show how well you can write. You should try to express your thoughts clearly. How well you write is much more important than how much you write, but you need to say enough for a reader to understand what you mean.

You will probably want to write more than a short paragraph. You should also be aware that a copy of your essay will be sent to each school that will be receiving your test results. You are to write only in the appropriate section of the answer sheet. Please write or print so that your writing may be read by someone who is not familiar with your handwriting.

You may make notes and plan your essay on the reverse side of the page. Allow enough time to copy the final form onto your answer sheet. You must copy the essay topic onto your answer sheet, on page 36, in the box provided.

Please remember to write only the final draft of the essay on pages 36-37 of your answer sheet and to write it in blue or black pen. Again, you may use cursive writing or you may print. Only pages 36-37 will be sent to the schools.

Directions continue on the next page.

REMINDER: Please write this essay topic on the first few lines of the first page of your essay sheet.

Essay Topic

If you could be an expert about any one subject, what subject would you pick? Explain your choice.

- Only write on this essay question
- Only pages 36 and 37 will be sent to the schools
- Only write in blue or black pen

NOTES

PRACTICE TEST 2

MIDDLE LEVEL

HOW TO TAKE THIS PRACTICE TEST

To simulate an accurate testing environment, sit at a desk in a quiet location free of distractions—no TV, computers, phones, music, or noise—and clear your desk of all materials except pencils and erasers. Remember that no calculators, rulers, protractors, dictionaries, or other aids are allowed on the ISEE.

Give yourself the following amounts of time for each section:

SECTION	SUBJECT	TIME LIMIT
1	Verbal Reasoning	20 minutes
2	Quantitative Reasoning	35 minutes
	5 minute break	
3	Reading Comprehension	35 minutes
4	Mathematics Achievement	40 minutes
	5 minute break	
5	Essay	30 minutes

Have an adult help you monitor your time, or use a watch and time yourself. Only give yourself the allotted time for each section; put your pencil down when your time is up.

Follow the instructions carefully. As you take your test, bubble your answers into the answer sheets provided. Use the test booklet as scratch paper for notes and calculations. Remember that you are not granted time at the end of a section to transfer your answers to the answer sheet, so you must do this as you go along.

When you are finished, check your answers against the answer keys provided. Then, score your exam using the directions at the end of the book.

Note: students with diagnosed learning disabilities who apply for testing with accommodations may receive extra time, or may be allowed to use certain assistive devices during the ISEE. For more information, visit http://erblearn.org/parents/admission/isee/accommodations.

Ivy Global

ISEE
MIDDLE LEVEL TEST 2

MARKING INSTRUCTIONS

- Use a #2 or HB pencil only on pages 82 and 83.
- Use a ballpoint pen for your essay on pages 84 and 85.
- Make dark marks that completely fill the circle.
- Erase clearly any mark you wish to change.
- Make no stray marks on this form.
- Do not fold or crease this form.

Correct Mark 

Incorrect Marks 

1 VERBAL REASONING

1 Ⓐ Ⓑ Ⓒ Ⓓ	15 Ⓐ Ⓑ Ⓒ Ⓓ	29 Ⓐ Ⓑ Ⓒ Ⓓ
2 Ⓐ Ⓑ Ⓒ Ⓓ	16 Ⓐ Ⓑ Ⓒ Ⓓ	30 Ⓐ Ⓑ Ⓒ Ⓓ
3 Ⓐ Ⓑ Ⓒ Ⓓ	17 Ⓐ Ⓑ Ⓒ Ⓓ	31 Ⓐ Ⓑ Ⓒ Ⓓ
4 Ⓐ Ⓑ Ⓒ Ⓓ	18 Ⓐ Ⓑ Ⓒ Ⓓ	32 Ⓐ Ⓑ Ⓒ Ⓓ
5 Ⓐ Ⓑ Ⓒ Ⓓ	19 Ⓐ Ⓑ Ⓒ Ⓓ	33 Ⓐ Ⓑ Ⓒ Ⓓ
6 Ⓐ Ⓑ Ⓒ Ⓓ	20 Ⓐ Ⓑ Ⓒ Ⓓ	34 Ⓐ Ⓑ Ⓒ Ⓓ Lower Level Ends
7 Ⓐ Ⓑ Ⓒ Ⓓ	21 Ⓐ Ⓑ Ⓒ Ⓓ	35 Ⓐ Ⓑ Ⓒ Ⓓ
8 Ⓐ Ⓑ Ⓒ Ⓓ	22 Ⓐ Ⓑ Ⓒ Ⓓ	36 Ⓐ Ⓑ Ⓒ Ⓓ
9 Ⓐ Ⓑ Ⓒ Ⓓ	23 Ⓐ Ⓑ Ⓒ Ⓓ	37 Ⓐ Ⓑ Ⓒ Ⓓ
10 Ⓐ Ⓑ Ⓒ Ⓓ	24 Ⓐ Ⓑ Ⓒ Ⓓ	38 Ⓐ Ⓑ Ⓒ Ⓓ
11 Ⓐ Ⓑ Ⓒ Ⓓ	25 Ⓐ Ⓑ Ⓒ Ⓓ	39 Ⓐ Ⓑ Ⓒ Ⓓ
12 Ⓐ Ⓑ Ⓒ Ⓓ	26 Ⓐ Ⓑ Ⓒ Ⓓ	40 Ⓐ Ⓑ Ⓒ Ⓓ Middle/Upper Level Ends
13 Ⓐ Ⓑ Ⓒ Ⓓ	27 Ⓐ Ⓑ Ⓒ Ⓓ	
14 Ⓐ Ⓑ Ⓒ Ⓓ	28 Ⓐ Ⓑ Ⓒ Ⓓ	

2 QUANTITATIVE REASONING

1	Ⓐ Ⓑ Ⓒ Ⓓ	15	Ⓐ Ⓑ Ⓒ Ⓓ	29	Ⓐ Ⓑ Ⓒ Ⓓ
2	Ⓐ Ⓑ Ⓒ Ⓓ	16	Ⓐ Ⓑ Ⓒ Ⓓ	30	Ⓐ Ⓑ Ⓒ Ⓓ
3	Ⓐ Ⓑ Ⓒ Ⓓ	17	Ⓐ Ⓑ Ⓒ Ⓓ	31	Ⓐ Ⓑ Ⓒ Ⓓ
4	Ⓐ Ⓑ Ⓒ Ⓓ	18	Ⓐ Ⓑ Ⓒ Ⓓ	32	Ⓐ Ⓑ Ⓒ Ⓓ
5	Ⓐ Ⓑ Ⓒ Ⓓ	19	Ⓐ Ⓑ Ⓒ Ⓓ	33	Ⓐ Ⓑ Ⓒ Ⓓ
6	Ⓐ Ⓑ Ⓒ Ⓓ	20	Ⓐ Ⓑ Ⓒ Ⓓ	34	Ⓐ Ⓑ Ⓒ Ⓓ
7	Ⓐ Ⓑ Ⓒ Ⓓ	21	Ⓐ Ⓑ Ⓒ Ⓓ	35	Ⓐ Ⓑ Ⓒ Ⓓ
8	Ⓐ Ⓑ Ⓒ Ⓓ	22	Ⓐ Ⓑ Ⓒ Ⓓ	36	Ⓐ Ⓑ Ⓒ Ⓓ
9	Ⓐ Ⓑ Ⓒ Ⓓ	23	Ⓐ Ⓑ Ⓒ Ⓓ	37	Ⓐ Ⓑ Ⓒ Ⓓ Middle/Upper Level Ends
10	Ⓐ Ⓑ Ⓒ Ⓓ	24	Ⓐ Ⓑ Ⓒ Ⓓ	38	Ⓐ Ⓑ Ⓒ Ⓓ Lower Level Ends
11	Ⓐ Ⓑ Ⓒ Ⓓ	25	Ⓐ Ⓑ Ⓒ Ⓓ		
12	Ⓐ Ⓑ Ⓒ Ⓓ	26	Ⓐ Ⓑ Ⓒ Ⓓ		
13	Ⓐ Ⓑ Ⓒ Ⓓ	27	Ⓐ Ⓑ Ⓒ Ⓓ		
14	Ⓐ Ⓑ Ⓒ Ⓓ	28	Ⓐ Ⓑ Ⓒ Ⓓ		

3 READING COMPREHENSION

1	Ⓐ Ⓑ Ⓒ Ⓓ	15	Ⓐ Ⓑ Ⓒ Ⓓ	29	Ⓐ Ⓑ Ⓒ Ⓓ
2	Ⓐ Ⓑ Ⓒ Ⓓ	16	Ⓐ Ⓑ Ⓒ Ⓓ	30	Ⓐ Ⓑ Ⓒ Ⓓ
3	Ⓐ Ⓑ Ⓒ Ⓓ	17	Ⓐ Ⓑ Ⓒ Ⓓ	31	Ⓐ Ⓑ Ⓒ Ⓓ
4	Ⓐ Ⓑ Ⓒ Ⓓ	18	Ⓐ Ⓑ Ⓒ Ⓓ	32	Ⓐ Ⓑ Ⓒ Ⓓ
5	Ⓐ Ⓑ Ⓒ Ⓓ	19	Ⓐ Ⓑ Ⓒ Ⓓ	33	Ⓐ Ⓑ Ⓒ Ⓓ
6	Ⓐ Ⓑ Ⓒ Ⓓ	20	Ⓐ Ⓑ Ⓒ Ⓓ	34	Ⓐ Ⓑ Ⓒ Ⓓ
7	Ⓐ Ⓑ Ⓒ Ⓓ	21	Ⓐ Ⓑ Ⓒ Ⓓ	35	Ⓐ Ⓑ Ⓒ Ⓓ
8	Ⓐ Ⓑ Ⓒ Ⓓ	22	Ⓐ Ⓑ Ⓒ Ⓓ	36	Ⓐ Ⓑ Ⓒ Ⓓ Middle/Upper Level Ends
9	Ⓐ Ⓑ Ⓒ Ⓓ	23	Ⓐ Ⓑ Ⓒ Ⓓ		
10	Ⓐ Ⓑ Ⓒ Ⓓ	24	Ⓐ Ⓑ Ⓒ Ⓓ		
11	Ⓐ Ⓑ Ⓒ Ⓓ	25	Ⓐ Ⓑ Ⓒ Ⓓ Lower Level Ends		
12	Ⓐ Ⓑ Ⓒ Ⓓ	26	Ⓐ Ⓑ Ⓒ Ⓓ		
13	Ⓐ Ⓑ Ⓒ Ⓓ	27	Ⓐ Ⓑ Ⓒ Ⓓ		
14	Ⓐ Ⓑ Ⓒ Ⓓ	28	Ⓐ Ⓑ Ⓒ Ⓓ		

4 MATHEMATICS ACHIEVEMENT

1	Ⓐ Ⓑ Ⓒ Ⓓ	18	Ⓐ Ⓑ Ⓒ Ⓓ	35	Ⓐ Ⓑ Ⓒ Ⓓ
2	Ⓐ Ⓑ Ⓒ Ⓓ	19	Ⓐ Ⓑ Ⓒ Ⓓ	36	Ⓐ Ⓑ Ⓒ Ⓓ
3	Ⓐ Ⓑ Ⓒ Ⓓ	20	Ⓐ Ⓑ Ⓒ Ⓓ	37	Ⓐ Ⓑ Ⓒ Ⓓ
4	Ⓐ Ⓑ Ⓒ Ⓓ	21	Ⓐ Ⓑ Ⓒ Ⓓ	38	Ⓐ Ⓑ Ⓒ Ⓓ
5	Ⓐ Ⓑ Ⓒ Ⓓ	22	Ⓐ Ⓑ Ⓒ Ⓓ	39	Ⓐ Ⓑ Ⓒ Ⓓ
6	Ⓐ Ⓑ Ⓒ Ⓓ	23	Ⓐ Ⓑ Ⓒ Ⓓ	40	Ⓐ Ⓑ Ⓒ Ⓓ
7	Ⓐ Ⓑ Ⓒ Ⓓ	24	Ⓐ Ⓑ Ⓒ Ⓓ	41	Ⓐ Ⓑ Ⓒ Ⓓ
8	Ⓐ Ⓑ Ⓒ Ⓓ	25	Ⓐ Ⓑ Ⓒ Ⓓ	42	Ⓐ Ⓑ Ⓒ Ⓓ
9	Ⓐ Ⓑ Ⓒ Ⓓ	26	Ⓐ Ⓑ Ⓒ Ⓓ	43	Ⓐ Ⓑ Ⓒ Ⓓ
10	Ⓐ Ⓑ Ⓒ Ⓓ	27	Ⓐ Ⓑ Ⓒ Ⓓ	44	Ⓐ Ⓑ Ⓒ Ⓓ
11	Ⓐ Ⓑ Ⓒ Ⓓ	28	Ⓐ Ⓑ Ⓒ Ⓓ	45	Ⓐ Ⓑ Ⓒ Ⓓ
12	Ⓐ Ⓑ Ⓒ Ⓓ	29	Ⓐ Ⓑ Ⓒ Ⓓ	46	Ⓐ Ⓑ Ⓒ Ⓓ
13	Ⓐ Ⓑ Ⓒ Ⓓ	30	Ⓐ Ⓑ Ⓒ Ⓓ Lower Level Ends	47	Ⓐ Ⓑ Ⓒ Ⓓ Middle/Upper Level Ends
14	Ⓐ Ⓑ Ⓒ Ⓓ	31	Ⓐ Ⓑ Ⓒ Ⓓ		
15	Ⓐ Ⓑ Ⓒ Ⓓ	32	Ⓐ Ⓑ Ⓒ Ⓓ		
16	Ⓐ Ⓑ Ⓒ Ⓓ	33	Ⓐ Ⓑ Ⓒ Ⓓ		
17	Ⓐ Ⓑ Ⓒ Ⓓ	34	Ⓐ Ⓑ Ⓒ Ⓓ		

STUDENT NAME ______________________ GRADE APPLYING FOR ________

Use a blue or black ballpoint pen to write the final draft of your essay on this sheet.

You must write your essay topic in this space.

Use specific details and examples in your response.

Section 1
Verbal Reasoning

40 Questions | Time: 20 minutes

This section is divided into two parts that contain two different types of questions. As soon as you have completed Part One, answer the questions in Part Two. You may write in your test booklet. For each answer you select, fill in the corresponding circle on your answer document.

PART ONE — SYNONYMS

Each question in Part One consists of a word in capital letters followed by four answer choices. Select the one word that is most nearly the same in meaning as the word in capital letters.

SAMPLE QUESTION: Sample Answer

CHARGE: Ⓐ Ⓑ ● Ⓓ

(A) release

(B) belittle

(C) accuse

(D) conspire

The correct answer is "accuse," so circle C is darkened.

PART TWO — SENTENCE COMPLETION

Each question in Part Two is made up of a sentence with one blank. Each blank indicates that a word is missing. The sentence is followed by four answer choices. Select the word that will best complete the meaning of the sentence as a whole.

SAMPLE QUESTION: Sample Answer

It rained so much that the streets were -------. ● Ⓑ Ⓒ Ⓓ

(A) flooded

(B) arid

(C) paved

(D) crowded

The correct answer is "flooded," so circle A is darkened.

STOP. Do not go on until told to do so.

PART ONE – SYNONYMS

Directions: Select the word that is most nearly the same in meaning as the word in capital letters.

1. IMPEDE
   (A) increase
   (B) ply
   (C) block
   (D) prepare

2. NOTORIOUS
   (A) masculine
   (B) gelatinous
   (C) infamous
   (D) numerous

3. EXUBERANT
   (A) magical
   (B) cheerful
   (C) slippery
   (D) exhausted

4. RIGID
   (A) thorough
   (B) direct
   (C) cold
   (D) inflexible

5. MOPE
   (A) polish
   (B) sleep
   (C) pout
   (D) attempt

6. EAGER
   (A) thoughtful
   (B) bored
   (C) enthusiastic
   (D) inspired

7. DREGS
   (A) remnants
   (B) coffee
   (C) fighters
   (D) surplus

8. PROBABLE
   (A) soft
   (B) likely
   (C) distinct
   (D) detestable

9. VARIABLE
   (A) vertical
   (B) capable
   (C) colorful
   (D) changeable

10. ANNUL
   (A) record
   (B) celebrate
   (C) subtract
   (D) void

Go on to the next page ➡

11. MERCILESS
    (A) thankless
    (B) insecure
    (C) ruthless
    (D) aggressive

12. PUNGENT
    (A) acrid
    (B) unlikely
    (C) peripheral
    (D) wet

13. HUBRIS
    (A) arrogance
    (B) optimism
    (C) shame
    (D) indifference

14. DAWDLE
    (A) draw
    (B) hurry
    (C) stall
    (D) trip

15. IMMEDIATE
    (A) newsworthy
    (B) late
    (C) prompt
    (D) invisible

16. MOMENTOUS
    (A) decayed
    (B) damp
    (C) invincible
    (D) notable

17. SOLEMN
    (A) miserable
    (B) boring
    (C) magnificent
    (D) serious

18. SEIZE
    (A) attack
    (B) refuse
    (C) capture
    (D) count

19. MODERATE
    (A) partisan
    (B) measured
    (C) warm
    (D) careless

Go on to the next page ➡

PART TWO – SENTENCE COMPLETION

Directions: Select the word that best completes the sentence.

20. Sydney wanted her assignment to be very -------, so she spent two weeks working to answer every question completely.
    (A) anxious
    (B) delectable
    (C) thorough
    (D) nimble

21. Stephanie gained a reputation as a ------- student by joining clubs, making friends, and always introducing herself to new students.
    (A) defensible
    (B) gregarious
    (C) hostile
    (D) sturdy

22. Because of their --------, Edmund Hilary and Tenzing Norgay persisted in challenging circumstances and became the first pair of climbers to successfully ascend Mount Everest.
    (A) hesitation
    (B) anxiety
    (C) apprehension
    (D) tenacity

23. Mr. Blackburn put peanuts on his window sill to ------- the squirrels, whose company he enjoyed.
    (A) entice
    (B) deceive
    (C) confound
    (D) offend

24. I wrote down the titles of my favorite books as I finished them, and over a few weeks I ------- a list to share with my reading group.
    (A) compiled
    (B) damaged
    (C) measured
    (D) polished

25. Walt Disney turned to television to ------- Disney Land even before it was built, creating anticipation and excitement in advance of its grand opening.
    (A) dignify
    (B) exchange
    (C) construct
    (D) promote

26. The film *O Brother, Where Art Thou?* was ------- based on Homer's Odyssey; while there were many parallels, it was largely a new work.
    (A) falsely
    (B) loosely
    (C) entirely
    (D) quickly

27. Becoming an Olympic athlete requires tremendous -----------, as you must train consistently and keep competing even after tough losses.
    (A) respect
    (B) organization
    (C) dedication
    (D) trepidation

Go on to the next page ➡

28. Sections of the Appalachian Trail receive difficulty ratings for hikers; ------- should stay in the 1-4 range, leaving harder trails for more experienced hikers.
    (A) experts
    (B) adults
    (C) novices
    (D) climbers

29. Replicas sometimes ------- the original artwork so closely that only experts can tell them apart.
    (A) mitigate
    (B) confuse
    (C) repudiate
    (D) resemble

30. Jasper expressed his ------- to his collaborators by sending them each a small gift when the project was complete.
    (A) frustration
    (B) expectations
    (C) gratitude
    (D) anger

31. When police corruption is common, some citizens ------- the law, knowing that a small bribe can keep them out of trouble.
    (A) flout
    (B) uphold
    (C) enforce
    (D) impute

32. Conserving resources was ------- during World War I, as conservation was enforced by strict rationing laws.
    (A) undignified
    (B) permitted
    (C) compulsory
    (D) cursory

33. "Indorock" originated in the 1950s as a ------- of Indonesian and Western music, combining features of both styles.
    (A) conflict
    (B) charter
    (C) fusion
    (D) grounded

34. Even dogs that are normally docile can become ------- around their food, growling or even snapping at other dogs.
    (A) defensive
    (B) hoarse
    (C) poised
    (D) shabby

35. In a foreign lottery scam, the victim is ------- into paying a cash advance to claim a prize that doesn't exist.
    (A) arrested
    (B) bemused
    (C) assuaged
    (D) duped

36. Sailors have a number of traditional ------, including the beliefs that cats will bring good luck and that it is very bad luck to kill an albatross.
    (A) poems
    (B) superstitions
    (C) voyages
    (D) indiscretions

37. Katrina picked out a beautiful dress for her sister's wedding, but she had to ----it slightly for it to fit just right.
    (A) alter
    (B) design
    (C) create
    (D) reproduce

Go on to the next page ➡

38. Mrs. Baker wanted us to care about our work, so she had every student do an assignment on a topic that they --------- enjoyed
    (A) ironically
    (B) ostensibly
    (C) scarcely
    (D) sincerely

39. Many animals are becoming ---------- or extinct as their habitats are being destroyed.
    (A) abundant
    (B) endangered
    (C) domesticated
    (D) larger

40. The Companions were the ------- cavalry of the Macedonian army, so above all others they were given the best equipment, horses, and training.
    (A) elite
    (B) appalling
    (C) happiest
    (D) least

STOP. Do not go on until told to do so.

STOP

Section 2
Quantitative Reasoning

37 Questions | Time: 35 minutes

This section is divided into two parts that contain two different types of questions. As soon as you have completed Part One, answer the questions in Part Two. You may write in your test booklet. For each answer you select, remember to fill in the corresponding circle on your answer document.

Any figures that accompany the questions in this section may be assumed to be drawn as accurately as possible EXCEPT when it is stated that a particular figure is not drawn to scale. Letters such as x, y, and n stand for real numbers.

PART ONE — WORD PROBLEMS

Each question in Part One consists of a word problem followed by four answer choices. You may write in your test booklet; however, you may be able to solve many of these problems in your head. Next, look at the four answer choices given and select the best answer.

SAMPLE QUESTION: | Sample Answer

What is the value of the expression $3 + 7 \times (6 - 4)^2 - 8 \div 2$?

Ⓐ Ⓑ ● Ⓓ

(A) 14
(B) 16
(C) 27
(D) 32

The correct answer is 27, so circle C is darkened.

Go on to the next page ➡

QR

2

PART TWO — QUANTITATIVE COMPARISONS

All questions in Part Two are quantitative comparisons between the quantities shown in Column A and Column B. Using the information given in each question, compare the quantity in Column A to the quantity in Column B, and choose one of these four answer choices:

(A) The quantity in Column A is greater.

(B) The quantity in Column B is greater.

(C) The two quantities are equal.

(D) The relationship cannot be determined from the information given.

SAMPLE QUESTIONS:

Column A	Column B	Sample Answer
5	$\sqrt{25}$	Ⓐ Ⓑ ● Ⓓ

The quantity in Column A (5) is the same as the quantity in Column B (5), so circle C is darkened.

$x = 6^2 - 3 \times 4$

Column A	Column B	Sample Answer
x	22	● Ⓑ Ⓒ Ⓓ

The quantity in Column A (24) is greater than the quantity in Column B (22), so circle A is darkened.

STOP. Do not go on until told to do so.

STOP

1. Ivy is giving away rocks in the order of red, blue, yellow, gold, and silver. If Ivy keeps this color order and gives each of her friends 4 rocks, what color and order of rocks does she give to her 3rd friend?

   (A) red, blue, yellow, and gold

   (B) gold, silver, red, and blue

   (C) blue, yellow, gold, and silver

   (D) silver, red, blue, and yellow

2. If $b\bigstar = q \times \frac{3}{b} - b$, which expression is equivalent to $\frac{1}{5}\bigstar$?

   (A) $q\frac{1}{5}$

   (B) $q(15 - \frac{1}{5})$

   (C) $15q - \frac{1}{5}$

   (D) $15q - 1$

3. If Z is an integer less than -1, which of the following expressions has the largest value?

   (A) $-(Z + 24) - \frac{24}{Z^2}$

   (B) $-(Z - 24) - \frac{24}{-Z^2}$

   (C) $(Z + 24) - \frac{24}{Z^2}$

   (D) $(Z + 24) - \frac{24}{-Z^2}$

4. Li has 15 bookshelves that each measure 8 feet tall, 0.5 feet wide, and 4.5 feet long. She wants to store them in her closet, which measures 9 feet tall, 4 feet wide, and 5 feet long. How many bookshelves will she be able to fit inside the closet?

   (A) 4

   (B) 8

   (C) 10

   (D) 18

5. A family of n people is sharing an amount of rice that costs a total of $p \times n$. John and his brother each eat a $^1/_4$ of the total amount of rice. The total cost of the rice they ate was \$8.00. If each of the other family members splits the remaining rice equally and each has a portion that is $^1/_2$ the size of John's, what is the average cost of a serving of rice (p) per person in the family, rounded to the nearest penny?

   (A) \$2.00

   (B) \$2.67

   (C) \$8.00

   (D) \$16.02

6. A triangular block with a volume of 22.5 cm^3 is placed into a rectangular box, as shown below.

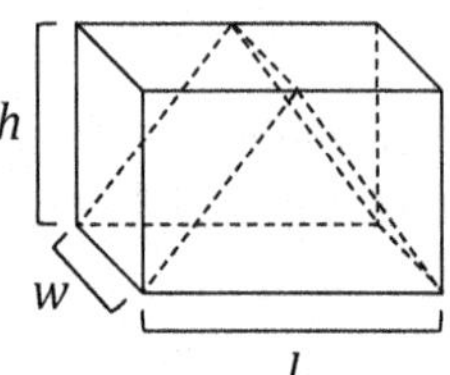

   If the box has a length (l) of 5 cm, a width (w) of 3 cm and a height (h) of 3 cm, what is the volume of the empty space remaining in the box?

   (A) $7\frac{1}{2}$ cm^3

   (B) $22\frac{1}{2}$ cm^3

   (C) $37\frac{1}{2}$ cm^3

   (D) 198 cm^3

Go on to the next page ➡

7. A series of pools in a row are connected to each other in a water park. There are 5 pools and each pool is one half of the size of the pool before it. If the largest pool is completely filled with w gallons of water, how much water is needed to completely fill all 5 pools?

(A) $w \times 2.5$ gallons

(B) $w \times 0.5^5$ gallons

(C) $w + w \times 0.5 + w \times 0.5^2 + w \times 0.5^3 + w \times 0.5^4$ gallons

(D) $w \times 0.5 + w \times 0.5^2 + w \times 0.5^3 + w \times 0.5^4 + w \times 0.5^5$ gallons

8. A cube is cut once horizontally and cut twice vertically, as shown by the dashed lines below, creating six rectangular pieces of equal size.

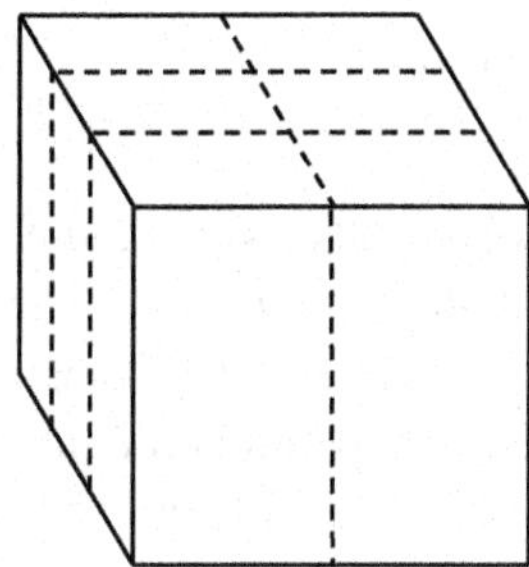

If one face of the cube has an area of 9cm^2, what is the volume of one of the six rectangular pieces?

(A) 3cm^3

(B) 4.5cm^3

(C) 9 cm^3

(D) 27cm^3

9. Malcolm is rolling one n-sided number polygon twice. Each side of the polygon is inscribed with a number 1 to n, and each number is used only once. What is the probability that the sum of his rolls will equal $2n$?

(A) $\frac{1}{n}$

(B) $\left(\frac{1}{n}\right)^2$

(C) n

(D) n^2

10. If $\boxed{a} = \frac{4}{3a} + 8$ what is $\boxed{2}$?

(A) $4\frac{2}{3}$

(B) $8\frac{2}{3}$

(C) $16\frac{2}{3}$

(D) $32\frac{2}{3}$

11. Each bicycle stores one spare wheel and each car stores three bicycles. If one flatbed truck can carry four cars and three spare wheels, what is the total number of spare wheels that can be carried by three flatbed trucks?

(A) 12

(B) 24

(C) 36

(D) 45

Go on to the next page ➡

12. If B is an odd integer and P is an even integer, which of the following is true?

    (A) The product of the smallest prime factor of P and the smallest prime factor of B is always an odd integer.

    (B) $\frac{P}{B}$ is never an integer.

    (C) $\frac{B}{2}$ is an integer.

    (D) $P \times B$ is always an even integer.

13. A recycling machine breaks down computers and uses the parts to manufacture widgets. Its results are represented in a table.

Computer(s) Recycled	Widgets Manufactured
1	$\frac{17}{3}$
3	?
5	$\frac{77}{3}$

Based on the table, how many widgets will the machine create when it recycles three computers?

    (A) $\frac{32}{3}$

    (B) 15

    (C) $\frac{47}{3}$

    (D) 17

14. If it takes 3 people 2 minutes to move 8 flagstones, how many people are required to move 16 flagstones in 3 minutes?

    (A) 4

    (B) 6

    (C) 12

    (D) 14

15. Timmy writes w words in a notebook on his first day. He writes again on the second day, adding 100% to the total number of words in his notebook. At the end of the week, he erases 50% of all the words written. How many words remain in his notebook?

    (A) $\frac{w}{2}$

    (B) w

    (C) $2w$

    (D) $4w$

16. Lorna rolls a six-sided number cube, labelled 1-6, twice. If she subtracts the value of her second roll from the value of her first, what is the probability that the difference will equal 3?

    (A) $\frac{1}{36}$

    (B) $\frac{1}{18}$

    (C) $\frac{1}{12}$

    (D) $\frac{1}{2}$

Go on to the next page ➡

17. The number of cars passing through an intersection during a five week period is shown below.

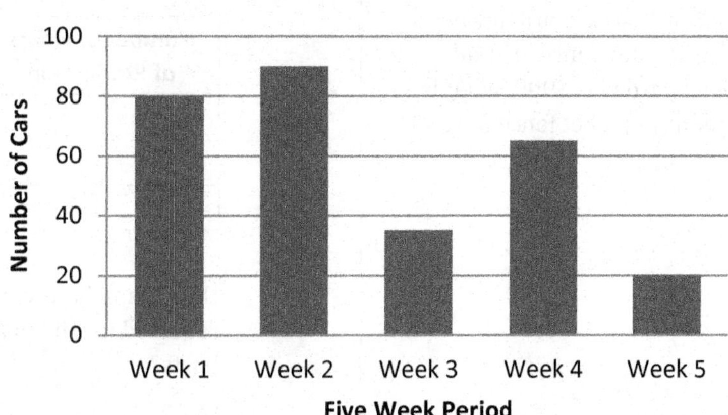

Which of the following statements for this period is true?

(A) The mode number of cars at the intersection for the five week period is 55

(B) The median number of cars over the 5 week period is equal to the number of cars during week 3

(C) Over the course of the 5 week period, the range of the number of cars at the intersection was 70

(D) The number of cars steadily diminished over the course of the 5 week period

---

18. Two lines are graphed.

Line A

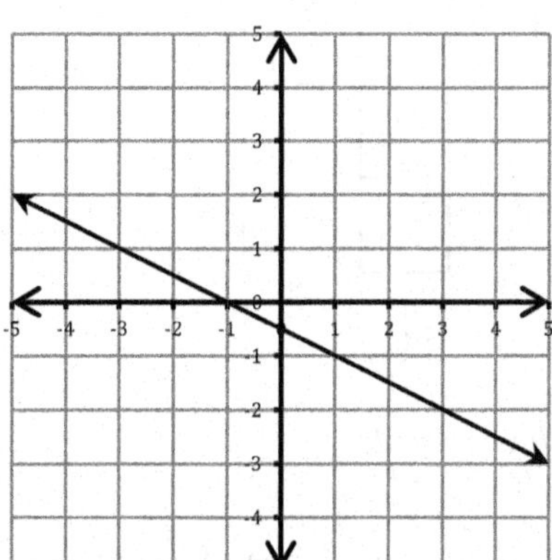

Line B

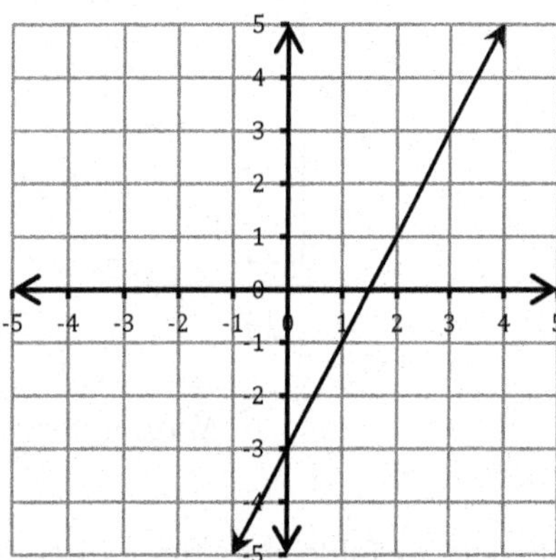

Which of the following statements is true?

(A) Line A is parallel to line B.

(B) Line A is perpendicular to line B.

(C) Line A is tangential to line B.

(D) Line A and line B both have negative slopes.

Go on to the next page ➡

19. Chen's backyard is one fourth the size of his neighbor's backyard. Both yards are squares. Chen is installing a picket fence along the border of his backyard. If the cost of installing a picket fence around Chen's neighbor's yard was $900, what is the cost of installing a picket fence around Chen's yard?

(A) $275

(B) $450

(C) $900

(D) $1800

20. A machine generates parts following the pattern shown in the table.

Number of Hours of Production	Number of Parts Created
2	3
4	9
6	27

How many hours of production are required for the machine to produce 81 parts?

(A) 7

(B) 8

(C) 9

(D) 12

21. Two nets are shown.

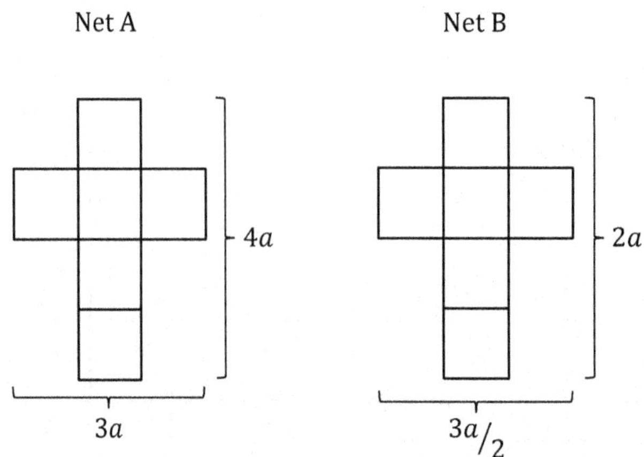

Note: Figures not drawn to scale.

When both nets are folded into three-dimensional objects, what will be the difference of the volume of object A minus the volume of object B?

(A) $\frac{a^3}{8}$

(B) $\frac{7}{8}a^3$

(C) a^3

(D) $8a^3$

Go on to the next page ➡

PART TWO – QUANTITATIVE COMPARISONS

Directions: Using the information given in each question, compare the quantity in column A to the quantity in Column B. All questions in Part Two have these answer choices:

(A) The quantity in Column A is greater.
(B) The quantity in Column B is greater.
(C) The two quantities are equal.
(D) The relationship cannot be determined from the information given.

	Column A	Column B
22.	$(5^1 - 1^5)^3$	125

A student graphs the line $3y = \frac{x}{2} + 3$

	Column A	Column B
23.	The slope of the line	The y-intercept of the line divided by 6

A shaded rectangle is placed within a square as shown.

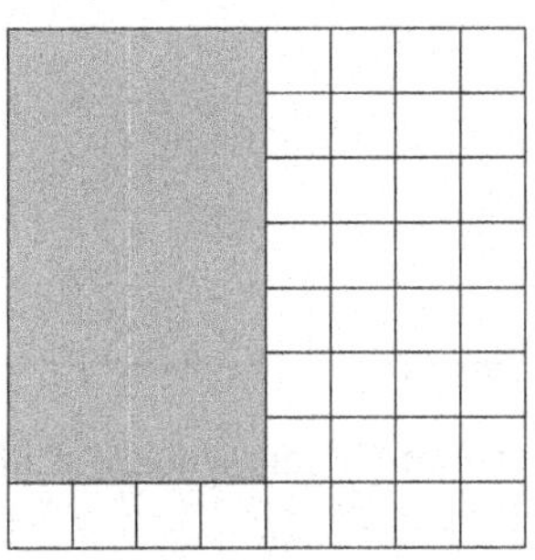

Note: The area of each square grid is equal to 1.

	Column A	Column B
24.	The non-shaded area remaining in the square	45

In Greentown every coin weighs 1 ounce regardless of its value. A shopkeeper in Greentown has $2.35 in her cash register, in quarters, dimes, and nickels.

One quarter = $0.25, one dime = $0.10, one nickel = $0.05

	Column A	Column B
25.	The minimum weight possible of the coins in the shopkeeper's cash register	8 ounces

An object with eight equal sides, numbered 1-8, is rolled twice and the results are recorded.

	Column A	Column B
26.	The probability that the sum of the rolls is equal to 15	$\frac{3}{64}$

A triangle has a hypotenuse that is 5 inches long and a leg that is 4 inches long.

	Column A	Column B
27.	The perimeter of the triangle in inches	13

Go on to the next page ➡

ANSWER CHOICES FOR ALL QUESTIONS ON THIS PAGE:

(A) The quantity in Column A is greater.
(B) The quantity in Column B is greater.
(C) The two quantities are equal.
(D) The relationship cannot be determined from the information given.

Roland has 6 peaches, 9 grapes, and 5 apples. He randomly selects 1 peach, 1 grape, and 1 apple.

	Column A	Column B
28.	The probability that Roland will select a white peach, a green grape, and a red apple	$\frac{1}{270}$

One bag of marbles provides enough marbles for 5 kids.

	Column A	Column B
29.	The number of bags of marbles needed for 105 kids	The number of kids provided for with $4\frac{2}{5}$ bags of marbles

The cost of a pencil is always 10% greater than the cost of an eraser.

	Column A	Column B
30.	The cost of a pencil if the cost of an eraser decreases by 10%	The original cost of an eraser

	Column A	Column B
31.	The slope of the line perpendicular to the line with coordinates of $(-3,3)$ and $(3,-3)$	1

A sample of students is randomly selected from two classrooms. Their weekly study habits are surveyed.

Classroom	**English**	**History**
Percent of classroom surveyed	40%	25%
People who study 1-5 hours per week	10	20
People who study 6+ hours per week	25	10

	Column A	Column B
32.	The predicted number of people who study 6+ hours per week for the entire English class	The predicted number of people who study 1-5 hours per week for the entire History class

Go on to the next page ➡

ANSWER CHOICES FOR ALL QUESTIONS ON THIS PAGE:

(A) The quantity in Column A is greater.
(B) The quantity in Column B is greater.
(C) The two quantities are equal.
(D) The relationship cannot be determined from the information given.

	Column A	Column B
33.	Distance A	Distance A

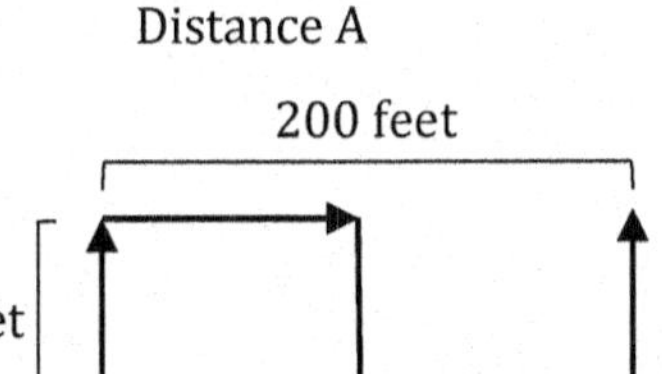

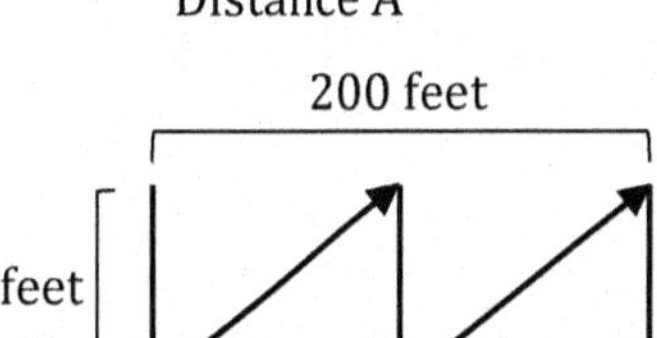

A deck of cards has 52 cards in total. There are 4 aces, 12 face cards, and 36 number cards. One card is picked and then replaced in the deck. The deck is shuffled and one more card is picked.

	Column A	Column B
34.	The probability of picking two number cards	$\frac{1}{2}$

	Column A	Column B
35.	$\dfrac{\sqrt{81}-3}{5-\sqrt{1+2\times 2^2}}$	-3

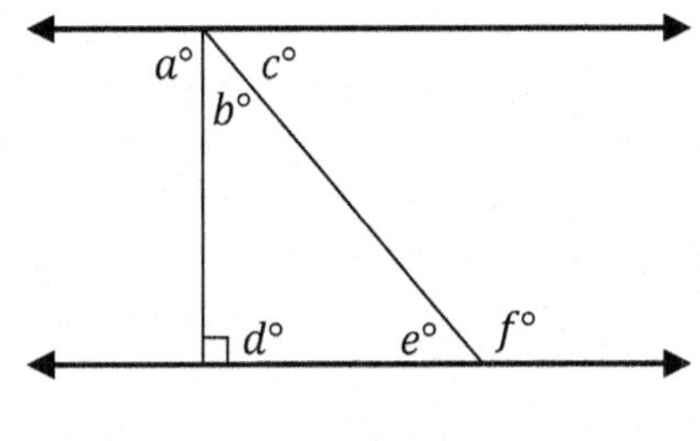

	Column A	Column B
36.	The sum of $a°$, $b°$, and $c°$	The sum of $a°$, $c°$, and $e°$

William is running across the Port Mann Bridge, which is 4,200 feet long, He stops at four locations on the bridge to take pictures. The distance from the beginning of the bridge to each of these points is calculated in the table below.

Stops Across the Port Mann Bridge	
Stops on the Bridge	**Distance from the Beginning of the Bridge**
A	1,530 feet
B	2,115 feet
C	3,500 feet
D	3,615 feet

	Column A	Column B
37.	The distance from William's *D* stop to the end of the bridge	The distance from William's *A* stop to William's *B* stop on the bridge

STOP. Do not go on until told to do so.

Section 3
Reading Comprehension

36 Questions | Time: 35 minutes

This section contains six short reading passages. Each passage is followed by six questions based on its content. Answer the questions following each passage on the basis of what is stated or implied in that passage. You may write in your test booklet.

STOP. Do not go on until told to do so.

Questions 1–6

In 1959, scientists in the Soviet Union who were interested in the process by which wolves became domesticated dogs initiated a breeding experiment using silver foxes. The experiment was led by Dmitri Belyaev, a Russian scientist and academian.

Belyaev believed that in the ancestral past of dogs, wolves with less fear of humans were more likely to live near them and eat scraps of their food. These wolves, he thought, must have interbred, passing down their tolerance of humans to their descendants, who eventually became domestic dogs. To mimic this process, he acquired a population of silver foxes and bred only those that had "low flight distance"—that is, the ones that he could get quite close to before they ran away from him.

Since behavior is rooted in biology, by choosing foxes that behaved in a certain way, Belyaev was choosing foxes that shared certain biological traits governing that behavior. After only a few generations of foxes chosen for breeding based on their "flight distance," Russian scientists observed notable changes in the behavior of their fox population. By just the tenth generation, Belyaev's foxes were not only more comfortable around humans than their wild forebears, but began actively seeking human attention- whining to be petted, as dogs do, and wagging their tails in response to a human presence.

There were also changes in the physical traits of the foxes. The color of their coats changed from the regular gray, white, and black pattern of wild silver foxes to a piebald pattern, resembling that of many domestic dogs. Many foxes were also born with floppy ears, in contrast to the pointy ears of their wild ancestors. These changes have been attributed to various causes; some speculate that the same physiological changes in the foxes which resulted in the changes to their behavior also cause changes to their physical appearance, while others have suggested that they were incidental changes, and simply occurred because there was no longer the same selection pressure as there had been in the wild to have a particular coat pattern.

The descendants of Belyaev's original experimental fox population are still alive today, and the project continues; however, since the collapse of the Soviet Union, the project has had to seek alternative sources of funding. One source of funding for the project has been the sale of some foxes as pets, and it is conceivable that one day owning a domestic fox may be as commonplace as owning a cat or dog.

Go on to the next page ➡

1. This passage answers all of the following questions EXCEPT which one?
   (A) During which year did Belyaev begin his silver fox experiment?
   (B) What did Belyaev believe was the process by which wolves became dogs?
   (C) Why did Belyaev choose to use silver foxes for his experiment?
   (D) Are there any differences between the domesticated foxes and their wild ancestors?

2. In line 45, the word "incidental" most nearly means
   (A) essential.
   (B) current.
   (C) chance.
   (D) pending.

3. Based on information in the passage, we can conclude that if one of Belyaev's foxes ran away from him as soon as it noticed him, Belyaev would
   (A) sell it to the Department of Fur Animal Breeding.
   (B) not use it to breed the next generation of foxes.
   (C) lose track of it in the lab.
   (D) breed it with a fox that had equally high "flight" distance.

4. This passage suggests that Belyaev's breeding experiment
   (A) has created foxes that are somewhat dog-like.
   (B) is unfair to the foxes.
   (C) is almost over.
   (D) failed to produce significant results.

5. Which best describes the way the passage is organized?
   (A) An argument is given, followed by a counterargument.
   (B) A theory examined and then is disproven by contradicting evidence.
   (C) A hypothesis is described, followed by a verifying experiment.
   (D) A problem is presented but no solution is given.

6. According to the passage, the causes of the physical changes in Belyaev's foxes
   (A) were a direct result of the changes observed in their behavior.
   (B) cannot be determined by scientists, because the original foxes are too different from their ancestors.
   (C) are not precisely known, although there are several possible explanations.
   (D) will eventually cause Belyaev's foxes to become indistinguishable from dogs.

Go on to the next page ➡

Questions 7-12

Sometimes geography can affect language in surprising ways. On the island of La Gomera—one of the Canary Islands off the cost of West Africa— deep ravines separate slivers of mountain terrain and the people who live on it. The ravines are too deep to be easily crossed, and too wide for shouted words to carry across them clearly. But the inhabitants of La Gomera developed a unique way of communicating across these deep ravines: an amazing whistled speech called Silbo Gomero. The sound of the whistles can be heard clearly across the ravines, allowing people to communicate in spite of the long distances between them. This whistled language is indigenous to the island, and its existence has been documented since Roman times.

The original whistled language was developed by the original inhabitants of the island, the Guanches. Though little is known about the original language spoken by the Guanches prior to Silbo Gomero, linguists believe that it must have been very simple for it to have been adopted into a whistled language. Once the Guanches developed Silbo Gomero, it spread to many other islands in the Canaries, including el Hierro, Tenerife, and Gran Canaria.

The modern language of Silbo Gomero is actually a dialect of Spanish. The Guanches originally converted the sounds of their own language into whistle-sounds, but eventually applied that practice to the language of the Spanish colonists. It is this whistled language that the Spaniards themselves adopted. Someone who speaks Silbo Gomero is often called a silbador, or "whistler."

Silbo Gomero was adopted by the Spanish settlers in the 16th century and survived after the Guanches' population dwindled. But with the advent of more modern forms of communication, a simple telephone could allow someone to communicate with others across the ravines, or anywhere else, without the aid of a whistled language. What was once a language of geographical necessity had become a cultural artifact.

People no longer needed to learn Silbo Gomero, and so fewer people did- and this unique means of communication was threatened with extinction at the dawn of the 21st century. But, having determined that this one-of-a-kind language was a piece of intangible cultural heritage worth preserving, the local government added it to the school curriculum.

Go on to the next page ➡

7. The primary subject of this passage is
   (A) the geography of La Gomera.
   (B) the Spanish occupation of the Canary Islands.
   (C) Silbo Gomero, the whistled language of La Gomera.
   (D) languages that involve whistling and other non-vocal sounds.

8. In line 15, the word "indigenous" most nearly means
   (A) fashionable.
   (B) native.
   (C) ancient.
   (D) religious.

9. Silbo Gomero was developed by the inhabitants of La Gomera so they could
   (A) plot against the Spanish colonists.
   (B) communicate better in the local terrain.
   (C) communicate with Spanish settlers.
   (D) enhance La Gomera's unique culture.

10. It can be inferred that many modern speakers of Silbo Gomero
    (A) use it for coded communication.
    (B) also speak some of the original Guanches language.
    (C) learned the language for cultural reasons rather than as a necessity.
    (D) have little interest in preserving the language for future generations.

11. How did the original Spanish settlers acquire Silbo Gomero?
    (A) They learned it in the schools of La Gomera.
    (B) They were the original settlers of La Gomera and invented the language.
    (C) They picked up the whistled form of Spanish that the Guanches had invented.
    (D) They began whistling in order to communicate better with the Guanches.

12. It can be inferred that La Gomera's ravines
    (A) were detrimental to the family units of La Gomera
    (B) helped give rise to a new language
    (C) caused conflict among the inhabitants
    (D) confused the Spanish colonists

Go on to the next page ➡

Questions 13-18

The Paleozoic ocean was dominated by animals known as nautiloids. With over 2,500 species, these marine cephalopods were the main predators of the period, and were characterized by a tough external shell. In many species, the shell served not only as a form of protection, but also as a form of buoyancy control. The modern nautilus, for example—one of few surviving nautiloids—has a shell containing air-filled pockets, which help it to maintain neutral buoyancy in water. While there used to be many types of shell shapes and forms, today there is only the spiral-shaped shell of the modern nautilus.

Much of what we know about extinct nautiloids actually comes from studying the modern nautilus. As one of only a few species of nautiloids that is still around today, nautili share many characteristics with their extinct ancestors. For example, the modern nautilus is also a predator, using its beak-like jaws to feed on crustaceans. The modern nautilus also uses the same mechanism for movement as its ancestors: jet propulsion. When the nautilus wants to move in a certain direction, it points an interior funnel in the desired direction and expels water from it, propelling it forward. The combination of its air-filled pockets and jet propulsion allows the nautilus to move easily through the ocean.

Unlike the nautilus, many other modern cephalopods lack an external shell, but the shell usually isn't completely absent. Instead, modern cephalopods often possess an internal shell. In cuttlefish this shell is called the cuttlebone and, like the shell of the nautilus, contains gas-filled pockets that help the cuttlefish to maintain buoyancy. It is this cuttlebone that distinguishes cuttlefish from other squid species, which they closely resemble. Squid have lost their ancestral shells entirely over the course of their evolution; they now only have a pen, a small internal structure where muscles attach. Since they lack a shell with gas pockets, squid species must use other physical traits to maintain neutral buoyancy, such as producing internal liquid ammonia that is lighter than water.

Go on to the next page ➡

13. In this passage, the author's main purpose is to
    (A) entertain.
    (B) speculate.
    (C) inform.
    (D) inquire.

14. Nautilus shells contain gas-filled pockets
    (A) for the storage of food.
    (B) for buoyancy control.
    (C) to eliminate waste.
    (D) for protection from predators.

15. In line 39, the word "distinguishes" most nearly means
    (A) differentiates.
    (B) honors.
    (C) poses.
    (D) outlines.

16. Based on the context of the passage, the word "cephalopod" (line 3) most likely refers to
    (A) any animal with a shell.
    (B) any marine predator.
    (C) a subset of nautiloids, some of which survive in the modern day.
    (D) a broader category of animals which includes the nautiloids.

17. It can be inferred from the passage that most nautiloids
    (A) possessed internal shells.
    (B) hunted other nautiloids.
    (C) are now extinct.
    (D) could not swim.

18. In line 27, the word "expels" most nearly means
    (A) tricks.
    (B) entraps.
    (C) ejects.
    (D) inhales.

Go on to the next page ➡

Questions 19-24

The air out there was different from home; the air of home was cool and humid, but here the hot, dry air pulled the moisture from your skin. The trees were different, too – stunted things, with short, gnarly bodies, and only sparse needles for their foliage. The ground was parched, and the rocks were not the familiar greys and greens of the moist and mossy boulders of home, but yellow and orange, and dotted here and there with lichens of black, and white, and red. We hiked for a little more than an hour in that alien landscape, and then we came to the cliff which had been our destination.

We stood together at the top of the cliff, enjoying the gentle breeze. A hawk hovered in the distance, riding the updrafts. In the vast expanse before us, the only sound was the wind. We spoke in whispers, and she said, "It's so quiet."

"I know," came my reply. Somehow those words didn't seem like enough, so I added, "I bet if I shouted, it would echo for miles."

Turning to me with a mischievous expression, she asked, "Why don't you?"

I thought about it. Why not? It didn't seem like there would be anything wrong with shouting, and there was nobody around who would stop me or complain that I had. I also thought that it could be fun to make such a sound, and to hear my voice echo back from the canyon. But the most pressing reason, although I am ashamed to admit it, was that it seemed as though I had been challenged. And so, with my ego at stake, I resolved to let out a resounding cry and make the canyon echo with my voice. But as I took a breath, something restrained me.

There was a sacred quality in the vast depth of the silence, and it affected me. An aversion to blasphemy welled up inside me, and I could not compel myself to shatter the peace of the moment. I exhaled quietly, and as my breath mingled with the passing breeze I confessed, "I don't think I should. It seems wrong."

"I know," she said, and we stood there a while longer without speaking. Eventually, we left the silence of the cliff and headed back to the trail; but the silence never left me—not entirely. In a peaceful moment, I can still hear it—and I still can't bring myself to break it.

Go on to the next page ➡

19. Why did the narrator refrain from shouting?

    (A) He didn't want to disturb a peaceful moment.

    (B) He was embarrassed to think that someone might hear him.

    (C) He was afraid that he would fail to live up to a challenge.

    (D) He was concerned that he might frighten the hawk.

20. Based on the context of the passage, "riding the updrafts" (line 17) probably means that the hawk was

    (A) hunting its prey

    (B) diving from the sky

    (C) calling to its mate

    (D) gliding on the wind

21. What does the narrator mean when he says "the silence never left me" (line 60)?

    (A) He was struck deaf.

    (B) He is able to ignore loud noises by remembering the silence.

    (C) He is still affected by the memory of the silence.

    (D) He is now attracted to quiet places.

22. In line 12, the word "alien" most nearly means

    (A) beautiful.

    (B) extraterrestrial.

    (C) unfamiliar.

    (D) deserted.

23. Which word best describes the narrator's attitude towards the silence of the cliff?

    (A) reverent

    (B) resentful

    (C) submissive

    (D) confused

24. It can be inferred that the narrator

    (A) hates hiking.

    (B) only went to the cliff to impress his friend.

    (C) is not originally from the area he is describing.

    (D) is scared of loud noises.

Go on to the next page ➡

Questions 25-30

Falconry—the practice of hunting with trained birds of prey—was for many centuries one of the main sports of the richer classes. The time, money, and hunting space that the sport required essentially ensured that only the noble classes would be able to participate. Since many more efficient methods of hunting have always existed, falconry has probably always been considered pure sport rather than a practical method of hunting. In this way, falconry became a status symbol for wealth and nobility; the lower classes could not afford to pursue inefficient food-gathering practices.

Falconry is quite ancient. It was introduced into England from continental Europe about A.D. 860, and from that time to the middle of the 17th century, falconry excited more enthusiasm than any other English sport, even fox-hunting. Stringent laws, notably during the reigns of William the Conqueror, Edward III, Henry VIII and Elizabeth I, were passed from time to time to regulate falconry. Different species of falcon and hawk were allotted to men according to rank and station—for instance, to the emperor the eagle and vulture, to royalty the jerfalcons, to an earl the peregrine, to a yeoman the goshawk, and to a servant the useless kestrel.

Falconry remained very popular until the 17th century, at which point guns became the preferred tool for hunting. Falconry continued to decline until it had a sudden resurgence during the late 19th and early 20th centuries. It was during this resurgence that falconry came to North America, where Colonel R. Luff Meredith helped to establish falconry as an American sport.

In modern times, technology and advances in veterinary medicine have expanded the range of the sport. For example, by attaching radio transmitters to the birds, falconers can pursue prey and engage in styles of flight that previously would have resulted in the loss of the falconry bird. Modern veterinary practices have also extended the life span of the birds.

Go on to the next page ➡

25. The main purpose of this passage is to
    (A) criticize the inefficient practice of using falcons to capture game.
    (B) provide some historical information about falconry.
    (C) argue that falconry is the best sport.
    (D) rank varieties of falcon and hawk.

26. As it is used in the passage, "pure sport" (line 9) is probably
    (A) a sport that only the wealthy engage in.
    (B) a sport that is favored and regulated by British monarchs.
    (C) a sport that is engaged in for entertainment and not out of necessity.
    (D) a very popular sport.

27. According to the passage, falconry most likely spread to England
    (A) in the middle of the 17th century.
    (B) during the reign of Queen Elizabeth.
    (C) around A.D. 860.
    (D) in order to help identify rank.

28. The passage suggests that fox-hunting
    (A) has been extremely popular in England.
    (B) is a cruel sport.
    (C) is the most effective way of capturing game.
    (D) is older than falconry.

29. Which of these puts the falcons and hawks in correct order of rank, from lowest to highest?
    (A) kestrel, vulture, goshawk, peregrine
    (B) eagle, peregrine, kestrel, jerfalcon
    (C) eagle, vulture, goshawk, peregrine
    (D) kestrel, peregrine, jerfalcon, eagle

30. In line 19, the word "stringent" most nearly means
    (A) flexible.
    (B) restrictive.
    (C) out-dated.
    (D) unnecessary.

Go on to the next page ➡

Questions 31-36

Rapid industrialization in China over past decades has led to dramatic increases in pollution. China's industrial revolution did not begin until the middle of the 20th century, far after western industrialization, but it occurred at a pace that far exceeded that of the western process. As a result, China leapt into the industrial world in only a single generation. While this process brought rapid economic growth, it also left China with a large industrial sector and few environmental protections.

Chinese environmental officials are now raising the same concern that has worried environmental activists for years: that severe pollution has led to a rise of so-called "cancer villages." Activists and some journalists have been using this term for several years to describe villages with high cancer rates which are located close to contaminated waterways, industrial parks, or construction sites.

A report issued this week by China's Environment Ministry specifically mentions "cancer villages," blaming the problem on severe water and air pollution. It is thought to be one of the first times the term has been used by government officials. Official statistics indicate that China has about 1,700 water pollution accidents each year and that up to 40 percent of the country's rivers are seriously polluted.

Water researcher Zhao Feihong at the Beijing Healthcare Association said last month that of the more than 100 rivers in Beijing only two or three can be used for tap water. "The rest of the rivers, if they have not dried up, are polluted by discharge," she said. She felt that the increased reporting from government officials on water pollution was a positive development, but that citizens would benefit from even more frequent disclosure of any environmental issues.

Air pollution is also a serious concern. During the last week of January, smog hung over cities and towns from Liaoning in the north to as far south as Guangdong, and air pollution reached unhealthy levels for long periods of time. Chinese officials blamed industrial activity, construction, and the widespread use of coal for heat.

Go on to the next page ➡

31. It can be inferred from the passage that heavy pollution
    (A) occurs mainly around small villages.
    (B) causes an increase in cancer rates.
    (C) is only a problem in China.
    (D) increases the demand for heating coal.

32. The passage was most likely taken from
    (A) a newspaper.
    (B) an encyclopedia.
    (C) a diary.
    (D) a letter.

33. The passage discusses all of the following as possible causes for high rates of cancer in "cancer villages" EXCEPT
    (A) water pollution.
    (B) pollutants from construction.
    (C) unhealthy lifestyle choices.
    (D) air pollution.

34. What would the author most likely discuss next?
    (A) the Chinese medical system
    (B) the various ministries in the Chinese government
    (C) why some rivers cannot be used for tap water
    (D) possible solutions for the problem of "cancer villages"

35. The primary purpose of the passage is to
    (A) recount China's industrial revolution.
    (B) discuss China's pollution and its effects on health.
    (C) describe Beijing's polluted rivers.
    (D) explain the role of China's environmental officials.

36. According to the passage, Chinese environmental officials are discussing concerns about "cancer villages"
    (A) long after environmental groups noticed the problem.
    (B) together with environmental activists and village leaders.
    (C) only after intense pressure by protest groups.
    (D) in hopes of drawing attention to a new and surprising problem.

STOP. Do not go on until told to do so.

SECTION 4
Mathematics Achievement

47 Questions | **Time: 40 minutes**

Each question is followed by four suggested answers. Read each question and then decide which one of the four suggested answers is best.

Find the row of spaces on your answer document that has the same number as the question. In this row, mark the space having the same letter as the answer you have chosen. You may write in your test booklet.

SAMPLE QUESTION:

Sample Answer

If $a = 3$, what is the value $a^2 + (3 \times 4) \div 6$?

(A) 3.5

(B) 11

(C) 14.5

(D) 20

The correct answer is 11, so circle B is darkened.

STOP. Do not go on until told to do so.

STOP

1. Machines A and B produce boxes at the same rate, but machine A breaks down three times quicker than machine B. If machine B can produce P boxes before it breaks down, approximately how many boxes can machine A produce before it breaks down?

   (A) $25\% \times P$

   (B) $33\% \times P$

   (C) $100\% \times P$

   (D) $300\% \times P$

2. A cube has a side length of x and is cut into four pieces diagonally as shown.

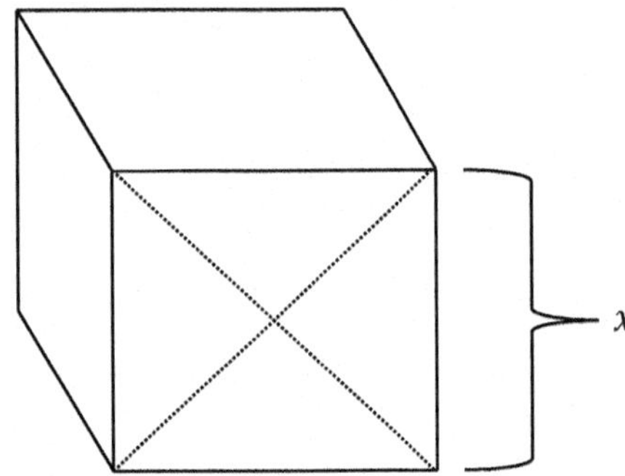

   What is the volume of one of these four sections?

   (A) $\frac{x^2}{4}$

   (B) $\frac{x^3}{4}$

   (C) x^2

   (D) x^3

3. If $A = \curvearrowleft \times 3$ and $Q = A \div 3$, which expression below is correct?

   (A) $Q = \curvearrowleft$

   (B) $Q = A \times 3$

   (C) $A = Q \times \curvearrowleft$

   (D) $A = Q \div 3$

4. At 80% capacity, five houses can hold 100 people. How many people can 3 houses hold at 100% capacity?

   (A) 50

   (B) 75

   (C) 100

   (D) 125

5. A mother needs to buy 2 boxes of baby wipes at \$9.00 each. There is a fee of \$5.00 for door-to-door delivery and a tax of 15% calculated after the delivery cost has been added. What is the total cost of the order?

   (A) \$20.70

   (B) \$23.00

   (C) \$25.70

   (D) \$26.45

6. If $A = \pi r^2$ and $r = {}^{d}/_{2}$ than what is A when d is 4 centimeters?

   (A) $\frac{1}{4}\pi$ cm²

   (B) $\frac{1}{2}\pi$ cm²

   (C) 4π cm²

   (D) 16π cm²

7. What is the difference of 6254 – 8926?

   (A) -2672

   (B) -2662

   (C) -2640

   (D) -2336

Go on to the next page ➡

Questions 8-9 use the following graph.

The number of births in Newville from 2009 to 2013 is shown on the graph below.

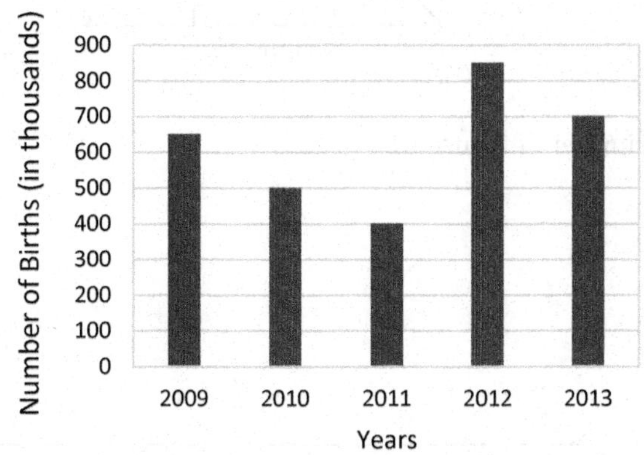

8. What is the median number of births per year in Newville?
   (A) 400,000
   (B) 500,000
   (C) 650,000
   (D) 700,000

9. What is the range of the number of births per year in Newville?
   (A) 4,500
   (B) 50,000
   (C) 300,000
   (D) 450,000

10. Norman is rolling two six-sided number cubes, numbered 1-6, and then multiplying the numbers together. What is the probability that the product of his rolls will be 12?
    (A) $\frac{1}{36}$
    (B) $\frac{1}{18}$
    (C) $\frac{1}{9}$
    (D) $\frac{1}{6}$

11. Giovanni writes one note for each of his two friends in the first period of school. His friends, in turn, each write notes for two of their friends in the second period. If this pattern continues until the fourth period of the school day, how many notes will be written in total?
    (A) 2
    (B) 16
    (C) 30
    (D) 64

12. If $g \times a = d$ and $e = \frac{g}{b} \div a$, which expression is equal to d?
    (A) $\frac{1}{b}$
    (B) ga^2
    (C) eba^2
    (D) $\frac{g}{ba}$

13. If $6A = 4$○ and ○ $= -3$, what is the value of A?
    (A) -12
    (B) -2
    (C) $\frac{3}{2}$
    (D) 4

Go on to the next page ➡

14. Figure CD is made from joining shapes D and C.

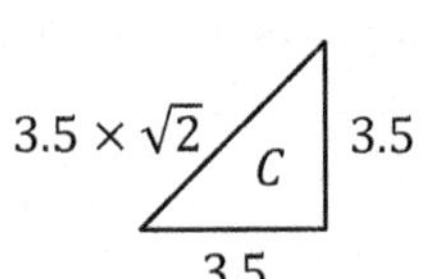

5
3.5 D 3.5
5

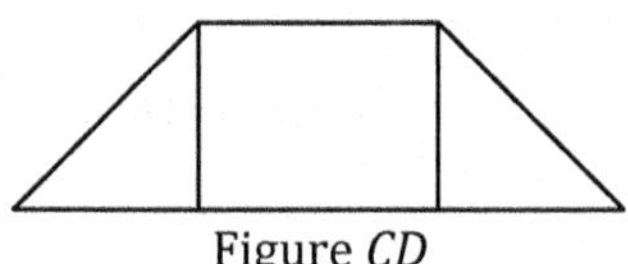
Figure CD

If C is a triangle and D is a rectangle, what is the perimeter of Figure CD?

(A) $23.5 + 3.5 \times \sqrt{2}$

(B) $17 + 7 \times \sqrt{2}$

(C) $31 + 7 \times \sqrt{2}$

(D) $34 + 7 \times \sqrt{2}$

---

15. If the ratio of $Y{:}\,4$ is the same as $132{:}\,44$, what is the value of Y?

(A) 8

(B) 12

(C) 16

(D) 32

16. James bought a box of 72 cookies. He first gave $^1/_2$ of the cookies to his brother, and then gave $^1/_3$ of the remaining cookies to his sister. If James gives 4 cookies to his mother, how many cookies will he have remaining in the box?

(A) 4

(B) 8

(C) 12

(D) 20

17. If a trapezoid has a base, b, of 2 centimeters, a top, t, of 6 centimeters, and a height, h, of 2 centimeters, what is the area of the trapezoid? Note: Area of a trapezoid $= \frac{1}{2}(b + t)h$

(A) 8 cm^2

(B) 10 cm^2

(C) 12 cm^2

(D) 16 cm^2

18. Fang is playing in a video game tournament, and has lost 3 games. Players receive a score of 0 for each game they lose, and a score of 1 for each game they win. With 5 games remaining, what is the minimum number of games that Fang must win if he wants his median score to be 1?

(A) 0

(B) 3

(C) 4

(D) 5

Go on to the next page ➡

19. Rachel has a bin of 9 socks with 3 red socks, 4 blue socks, 1 black sock, and 1 white sock. She selects one sock, puts it back and then selects one more. What is the probability that she will pick one red sock and then one black sock?

(A) $\frac{1}{27}$

(B) $\frac{1}{9}$

(C) $\frac{1}{3}$

(D) $\frac{4}{9}$

20. Which of the following is closest to 0.167×19?

(A) $\frac{1}{3}$ of 10

(B) $\frac{1}{6}$ of 40

(C) $\frac{1}{16}$ of 40

(D) $\frac{1}{3}$ of 20

21. The figure below shows a square with a side length of 5 inches and two identical rectangles whose areas are each 10 inches^2.

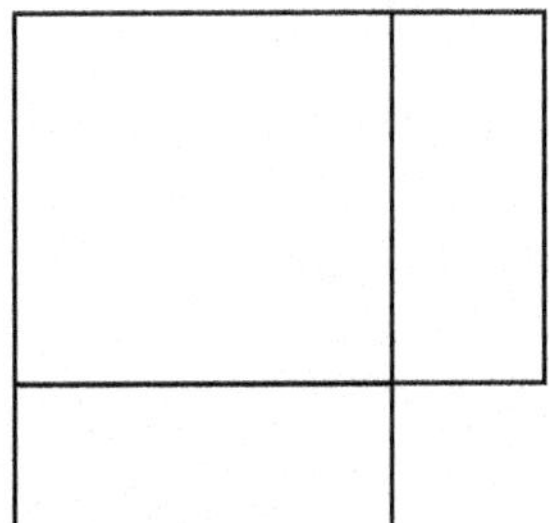

What is the perimeter of the entire figure?

(A) 18 inches

(B) 28 inches

(C) 38 inches

(D) 48 inches

22. Carl can drink 2 cups of milk in 2 minutes. If the rest of Carl's family can drink at the same rate, how many cups can the family of four drink in 3 minutes?

(A) 2

(B) 3

(C) 6

(D) 12

23. There are 48 butterflies in a box, and boxes of butterflies are stacked in a warehouse. If the ratio of boxes in the warehouse to butterflies in a box is 1:8, how many butterflies are in the whole warehouse?

(A) 44

(B) 88

(C) 288

(D) 384

24. In the figure below, a triangle is on top of two squares with side lengths of 6.

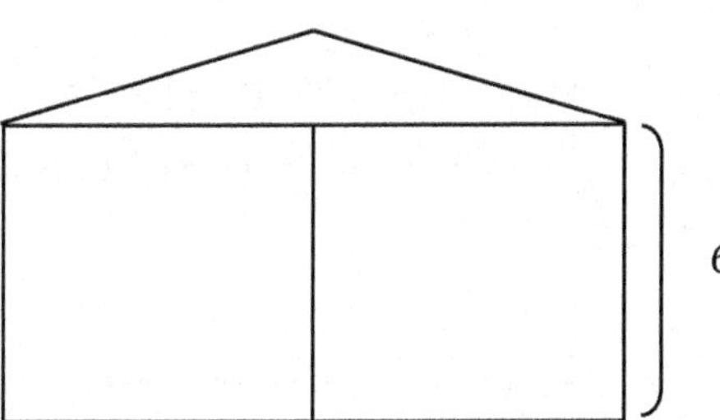

If the height of the entire figure is 10, what is its area?

(A) 48

(B) 60

(C) 96

(D) 120

Go on to the next page ➡

Questions 25-26 refer to the chart below:

John runs a 10 mile race. His time per mile as recorded at the end of each mile is shown on a line graph.

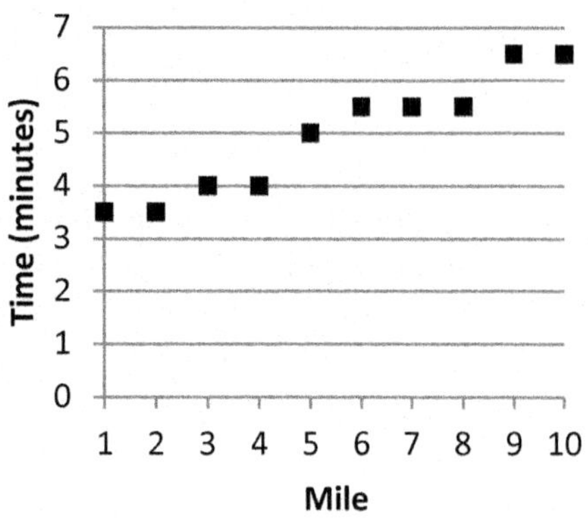

25. How many minutes does it take John to run the entire race?

    (A) 6.5
    (B) 48.5
    (C) 49.5
    (D) 50.0

26. Which of the following statements is true?

    (A) John's average (mean) time per mile was greater than his median time per mile.
    (B) John's median time was between 5 minutes and 5.5 minutes.
    (C) John's speed increased over the course of the race.
    (D) The mode for John's time per mile was 5 minutes.

27. A cement truck carries 216 cubic yards of mixed cement. A hole with a volume of 1620 cubic feet needs to be filled with cement. If the cement truck pours at a rate of 20 cubic yards per minute, how many minutes will it take for the pool to be entirely full?

    1 cubic yard=27 cubic feet

    (A) 1 minute
    (B) 2 minutes
    (C) 3 minutes
    (D) 4 minutes

28. On a set of blueprints for a house, 4 cm is equal to 3 meters. If the height of the house measures 12 cm on the blueprints, what is the actual height of the house?

    (A) 6 meters
    (B) 9 meters
    (C) 16 meters
    (D) 32 meters

29. Which is equivalent to the following expression?

$$3 \times \left(\frac{1}{2} - \frac{1}{3}\right) + \frac{3x}{12} = y$$

    (A) $x = -2(2y + 1)$
    (B) $x = -\frac{y}{4} + \frac{1}{2}$
    (C) $x = 4\left(y - \frac{7}{6}\right)$
    (D) $x = \frac{3}{2} + \frac{y}{4}$

Go on to the next page ➡

30. A flag pole is one third the height of an adjacent building, which is 16 meters tall. If a sapling is two eighths of the height of the flag pole, then how tall is it?

    (A) $\frac{1}{3}$ meters

    (B) $\frac{2}{3}$ meters

    (C) 1 meter

    (D) $\frac{4}{3}$ meters

31. What is the smallest prime factor of 143?

    (A) 1

    (B) 7

    (C) 11

    (D) 13

32. The number of bicycles produced during the months of June to November is shown on a graph.

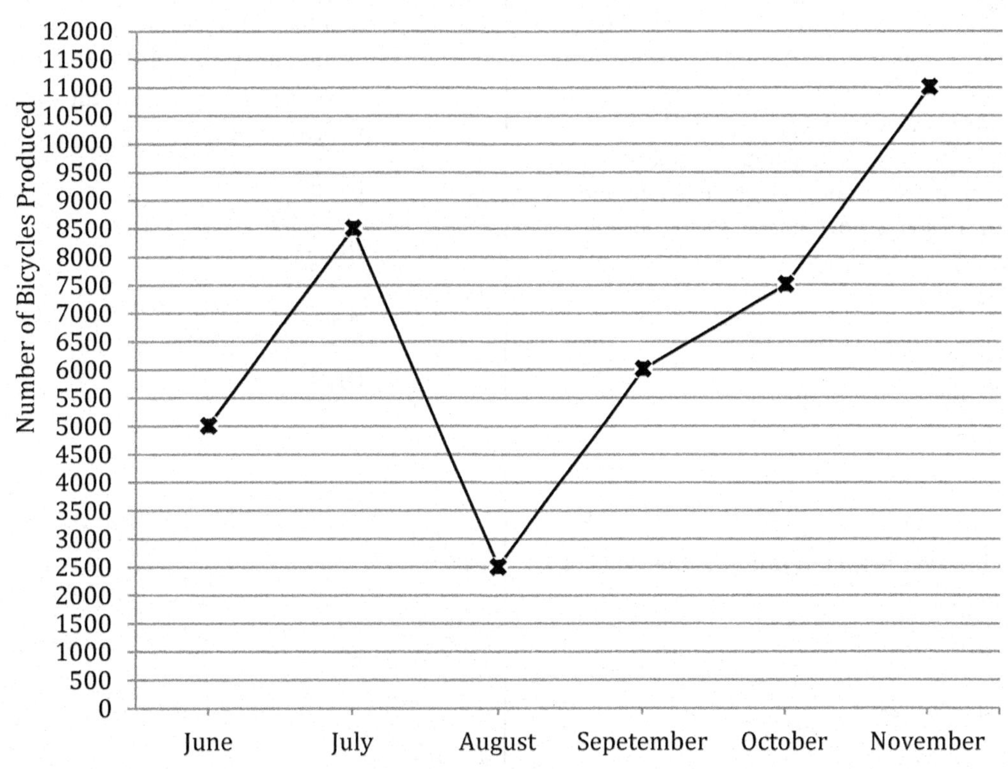

Which month showed the greatest percent increase in production from the month before?

(A) July

(B) September

(C) October

(D) November

Go on to the next page ➡

33. The sum of three consecutive integers is -9. What is the largest of the three integers?

(A) -9

(B) -6

(C) -4

(D) -2

34. If $\frac{\triangleleft}{3} = \square \times 4$ and $\square = 2$, what is the value of $\triangleleft$?

(A) $\frac{1}{12}$

(B) $\frac{1}{6}$

(C) $\frac{1}{3}$

(D) 24

35. Jordan has to decide between 5 different suits, 6 different hats, and 2 different pairs of socks. If he wants to select one outfit that has one suit, one hat, and one pair of socks, how many choices does he have?

(A) 13

(B) 30

(C) 60

(D) 120

36. For any numbers l and k, $\frac{l}{k} \times 2 = k + 4$. Which expression represents the value of $l \times 3$?

(A) $k \times 3$

(B) $\frac{3k^2}{2} + 6k$

(C) $\frac{3}{2}(k^2 + 2k)$

(D) $3(5k)$

37. What is the closest value to $\sqrt{78}$?

(A) 6

(B) 7

(C) 8

(D) 9

38. 40% of c is equal to r. What is 15% of r, in terms of c?

(A) $0.006c$

(B) $0.06c$

(C) $0.325c$

(D) $0.75c$

39. Christine is rolling one six-sided number cube, numbered 1-6, twice. If the first number rolled is the numerator and the second number rolled is the denominator, what is probability that the quotient of the two rolls is 2?

(A) $\frac{1}{36}$

(B) $\frac{1}{18}$

(C) $\frac{1}{12}$

(D) $\frac{1}{9}$

Go on to the next page ➡

40. Rashmi works for a computer company. The profit for the company, P, relates to the number of jobs, J, that she completes as per the equation below:

$$P = J \times \$200 - \$400$$

What does this formula indicate?

(A) For every project completed, the company gains $400.

(B) If no projects are completed, the company will not pay Rashmi.

(C) If Rashmi completes more than two projects for the company, the company will have a positive profit.

(D) Regardless of how many projects Rashmi completes, the company will gain profit from her work.

41. The circumference of a circle touches the points (-1,-1) and (1,1) on a graph.

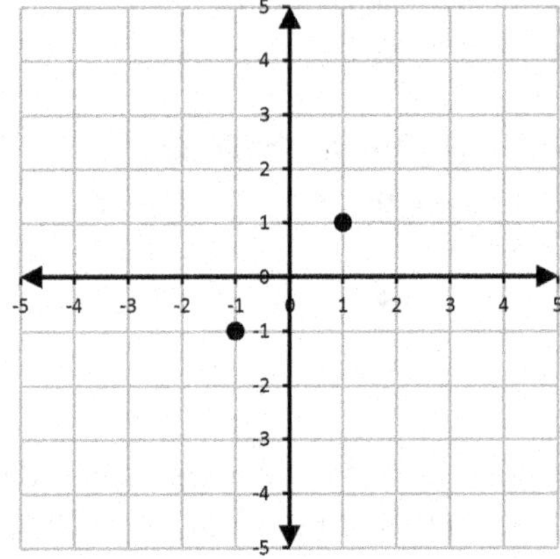

What is one other point on this graph that the circumference of this circle touches?

(A) (1,-2)

(B) (-1,2)

(C) (1,0)

(D) (1,-1)

42. In the coordinate plane below, if ΔABC were reflected along the x axis, what would be the new coordinates for point B?

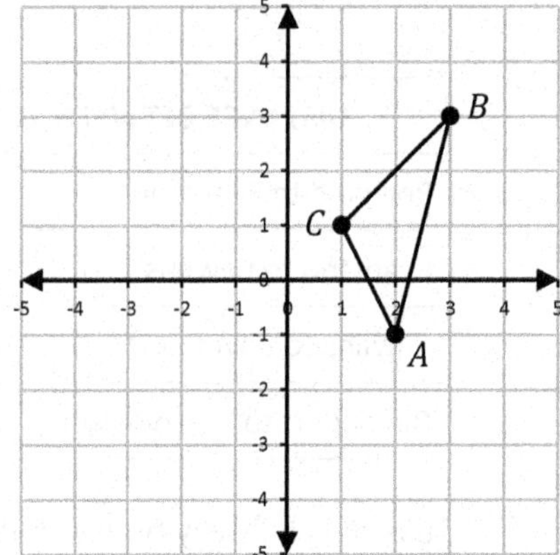

(A) (3,-3)

(B) (-3,3)

(C) (3,-2)

(D) (3,2)

43. $A = \frac{2}{(5-2)} \times \frac{4}{5} \times 3 - \frac{2(3+2)}{4}$

What is the value of A?

(A) $-\frac{17}{5}$

(B) $-\frac{9}{10}$

(C) $\frac{9}{10}$

(D) $\frac{23}{10}$

Go on to the next page ➡

44. Sasha is driving to Washington from Portland and must pass through four towns on her drive. The distances between each of these towns is represented in the table below.

DISTANCE BETWEEN TOWNS	
Portland to Evanston	805 miles
Evanston to Rawlins	208 miles
Rawlins to Davenport	944 miles
Davenport to Washington	843 miles

If Sasha is halfway between Rawlins and Davenport, which of the following is true?

(A) The total distance from Portland to Washington is 3,000 miles
(B) Sasha has 1,787 miles remaining to drive to Washington
(C) The distance from Portland to Rawlins is half the distance from Portland to Washington
(D) Sasha has driven more than half of the trip from Portland to Washington.

45. A trading card costs $3.00, and there is a 15% tax. Yun has a ten dollar bill and a five dollar bill. If Yun purchases three trading cards, how much change will he receive?

(A) $3.00
(B) $4.65
(C) $5.10
(D) $6.00

46. Continue the pattern:

(A) 

(B) 

(C) 

(D) 

47. Mama's Popcorn is estimating its profitability from sales. The cost to produce one bag of popcorn is $1.50 and each bag of popcorn sells for $4.00. The cost to set up in the market is $250.00 per day. If Mama's Popcorn expects to sell 150 bags of popcorn in a day, what will be its profit for the day after it pays all expenses?

(A) $125.00
(B) $225.00
(C) $250.00
(D) $600.00

STOP. Do not go on until told to do so.

Essay Topic Sheet

The directions for the Essay portion of the ISEE are printed in the box below. Use the pre-lined pages on pages 84-85 for this part of the Practice Test.

You will have 30 minutes to plan and write an essay on the topic printed on the other side of this page. **Do not write on another topic. An essay on another topic is not acceptable.**

The essay is designed to give you an opportunity to show how well you can write. You should try to express your thoughts clearly. How well you write is much more important than how much you write, but you need to say enough for a reader to understand what you mean.

You will probably want to write more than a short paragraph. You should also be aware that a copy of your essay will be sent to each school that will be receiving your test results. You are to write only in the appropriate section of the answer sheet. Please write or print so that your writing may be read by someone who is not familiar with your handwriting.

You may make notes and plan your essay on the reverse side of the page. Allow enough time to copy the final form onto your answer sheet. You must copy the essay topic onto your answer sheet, on page 84, in the box provided.

Please remember to write only the final draft of the essay on pages 84-85 of your answer sheet and to write it in blue or black pen. Again, you may use cursive writing or you may print. Only pages 84-85 will be sent to the schools.

Directions continue on the next page.

REMINDER: Please write this essay topic on the first few lines of the first page of your essay sheet.

Essay Topic

Tell us about someone who has had a major influence on the way that you think about the world, and explain how he or she has influenced your thinking.

- Only write on this essay question
- Only pages 84 and 85 will be sent to the schools
- Only write in blue or black pen

NOTES

ANSWER KEYS

CHAPTER 4

PRACTICE TEST 1

MIDDLE LEVEL

SECTION 1 – VERBAL REASONING (PAGES 39-43)

1. C	6. B	11. C	16. B	21. D	26. D	31. C	36. D
2. B	7. D	12. A	17. C	22. B	27. D	32. A	37. D
3. A	8. A	13. C	18. C	23. A	28. C	33. B	38. A
4. C	9. B	14. A	19. B	24. C	29. C	34. B	39. A
5. B	10. A	15. B	20. B	25. A	30. B	35. C	40. B

SECTION 2 – QUANTITATIVE REASONING (PAGES 46-53)

1. D	6. D	11. B	16. D	21. C	26. A	31. B	36. D
2. C	7. D	12. B	17. B	22. A	27. D	32. C	37. C
3. A	8. C	13. B	18. C	23. B	28. C	33. C	
4. A	9. C	14. B	19. B	24. B	29. B	34. B	
5. D	10. A	15. D	20. B	25. C	30. B	35. A	

SECTION 3 – READING COMPREHENSION (PAGES 55-66)

1. C	6. A	11. D	16. D	21. D	26. D	31. B	36. B
2. A	7. C	12. D	17. A	22. C	27. B	32. A	
3. B	8. B	13. C	18. A	23. A	28. B	33. D	
4. B	9. A	14. D	19. B	24. A	29. A	34. C	
5. C	10. A	15. A	20. B	25. A	30. D	35. D	

SECTION 4 – MATHEMATICS ACHIEVEMENT (PAGES 68-76)

1. B	7. D	13. B	19. A	25. C	31. A	37. D	43. B
2. D	8. D	14. C	20. D	26. B	32. B	38. B	44. D
3. A	9. D	15. A	21. B	27. B	33. C	39. D	45. B
4. C	10. C	16. B	22. A	28. B	34. B	40. C	46. A
5. D	11. B	17. B	23. A	29. C	35. B	41. B	47. C
6. B	12. D	18. C	24. C	30. D	36. B	42. D	

SCORING YOUR TEST

On the ISEE, you receive one point for every question you answered correctly, and you receive no points for questions you answered incorrectly or skipped. In each section, the ISEE also includes 5 or 6 experimental questions that do not count towards your score. You won't be told which questions are unscored, and for this reason, these practice tests do not have specific questions marked as experimental. This also means that it isn't possible to determine an exact score for each section of these practice tests, but you can estimate your score using the procedures below.

To estimate your **raw score** for your practice test, first count up the number of questions you answered correctly in each section. Then, follow the table below to subtract 5 or 6 points for each section, accounting for the experimental questions that would not be scored on your actual ISEE exam.

MY RAW SCORE			
Section	**# of Questions Correct**		**Raw Score**
Verbal Reasoning		– 5 =	
Quantitative Reasoning		– 5 =	
Reading Comprehension		– 6 =	
Mathematics Achievement		– 5 =	

SCALED SCORE

Once you have found your raw score, convert it into an approximate **scaled score** using the scoring charts that follow. These charts provide an estimated range for your ISEE scaled score based on your performance on this practice test. Keep in mind that this estimate may differ slightly from your scaled score when you take your actual ISEE exam, depending on the ISEE's specific scaling for that exam and any differences in your own test-taking process.

MIDDLE LEVEL SCALED SCORE RANGES				
Raw Score	**Verbal Reasoning**	**Quantitative Reasoning**	**Reading Comprehension**	**Mathematics Achievement**
42				875 – 905
41				875 – 905
40				870 – 900
39				870 – 900
38				865 – 895
37				865 – 895
36				860 – 890
35	895 – 925			860 – 890
34	890 – 920			855 – 885
33	890 – 920			855 – 885
32	885 – 915	895 – 925		850 – 880
31	885 – 915	895 – 925		850 – 880
30	880 – 910	890 – 920	915 – 940	845 – 875
29	875 – 905	885 – 915	910 – 940	845 – 875
28	875 – 905	885 – 915	905 – 935	845 – 875
27	870 – 900	880 – 910	905 – 935	840 – 870
26	865 – 895	875 – 905	900 – 930	840 – 870
25	865 – 895	875 – 905	895 – 925	835 – 865
24	860 – 890	870 – 900	890 – 920	835 – 865
23	855 – 885	865 – 895	885 – 915	830 – 860
22	855 – 885	865 – 895	885 – 915	830 – 860
21	850 – 880	860 – 890	880 – 910	825 – 855
20	845 – 875	855 – 885	875 – 905	825 – 855

19	845 – 875	855 – 885	870 – 900	820 – 850
18	840 – 870	850 – 880	870 – 900	820 – 850
17	835 – 865	845 – 875	865 – 895	815 – 845
16	835 – 865	845 – 875	860 – 890	815 – 845
15	830 – 860	840 – 870	855 – 885	810 – 840
14	825 – 855	835 – 865	855 – 885	810 – 840
13	825 – 855	835 – 865	850 – 880	805 – 835
12	820 – 850	830 – 860	845 – 875	805 – 835
11	815 – 845	830 – 860	840 – 870	800 – 830
10	815 – 845	825 – 855	835 – 865	800 – 830
9	810 – 840	820 – 850	835 – 865	795 – 825
8	810 – 840	820 – 850	830 – 860	795 – 825
7	805 – 835	815 – 845	825 – 855	790 – 820
6	800 – 830	810 – 840	820 – 850	790 – 820
5	800 – 830	810 – 840	820 – 850	785 – 815
4	795 – 825	805 – 835	815 – 845	785 – 815
3	790 – 820	800 – 830	810 – 840	780 – 810
2	790 – 820	800 – 830	805 – 835	780 – 810
1	785 – 815	795 – 825	805 – 835	775 – 805
0	780 – 810	790 – 820	800 – 830	775 – 805

PERCENTILE

When you take your actual ISEE exam, you will receive a **percentile** ranking comparing your performance against the performance of other students in the same grade who have taken the ISEE that year. For example, a percentile of 62 means that you scored higher than 62% of other ISEE test-takers applying to the same grade. Because your percentile ranking shows how well you performed according to your own grade level, these rankings are frequently given high consideration by admissions offices.

The following charts provide an estimate of your ISEE percentile rankings for this practice test, compared against other students applying to the same grade. For example, if you are scoring at or above the 75th percentile, you are scoring higher than 75% of other ISEE test-takers applying to the same grade. Keep in mind that these percentiles are estimates only, and your actual ISEE percentile will depend on the specific group of students taking the exam in your year.

MIDDLE LEVEL VERBAL REASONING PERCENTILES			
Grade Applying To	**75th percentile**	**50th percentile**	**25th percentile**
Grade 7	880	868	853
Grade 8	890	878	867

MIDDLE LEVEL QUANTITATIVE REASONING PERCENTILES			
Grade Applying To	**75th percentile**	**50th percentile**	**25th percentile**
Grade 7	877	865	853
Grade 8	884	873	864

MIDDLE LEVEL READING COMPREHENSION PERCENTILES			
Grade Applying To	**75th percentile**	**50th percentile**	**25th percentile**
Grade 7	885	869	850
Grade 8	897	883	868

MIDDLE LEVEL MATHEMATICS ACHIEVEMENT PERCENTILES			
Grade Applying To	**75th percentile**	**50th percentile**	**25th percentile**
Grade 7	882	871	861
Grade 8	886	876	867

STANINE

When you receive the score report for your actual ISEE exam, your percentile score will also be broken down into a **stanine**. A stanine is a number from 1-9 obtained by dividing the entire range of students' scores into 9 segments, as shown in the table below:

PERCENTILE RANK	STANINE
1 – 3	1
4 – 10	2
11 – 22	3
23 – 39	4
40 – 59	5
60 – 76	6
77 – 88	7
89 – 95	8
96 – 99	9

Although it isn't possible to calculate your exact stanine from this practice test, you can estimate a stanine score range by looking at your estimated percentile score on each section. For example, if you scored between the 50th and 75th percentile in one of your test sections, your stanine score would be between 5 and 6.

PRACTICE TEST 2

MIDDLE LEVEL

SECTION 1 – VERBAL REASONING (PAGES 87-91)

1. C 6. C 11. C 16. D 21. B 26. B 31. A 36. B
2. C 7. A 12. A 17. D 22. D 27. C 32. C 37. A
3. B 8. B 13. A 18. C 23. A 28. C 33. C 38. D
4. D 9. D 14. C 19. B 24. A 29. D 34. A 39. B
5. C 10. D 15. C 20. C 25. D 30. C 35. D 40. A

SECTION 2 – QUANTITATIVE REASONING (PAGES 94-101)

1. B 6. B 11. D 16. C 21. B 26. B 31. C 36. D
2. C 7. C 12. D 17. C 22. B 27. B 32. B 37. C
3. B 8. B 13. C 18. B 23. C 28. D 33. B
4. B 9. B 14. A 19. B 24. B 29. B 34. B
5. B 10. B 15. B 20. B 25. A 30. B 35. A

SECTION 3 – READING COMPREHENSION (PAGES 103-114)

1. C 6. C 11. C 16. D 21. C 26. C 31. B 36. A
2. C 7. C 12. B 17. C 22. C 27. C 32. A
3. B 8. B 13. C 18. C 23. A 28. A 33. C
4. A 9. B 14. B 19. A 24. C 29. D 34. D
5. C 10. C 15. A 20. D 25. B 30. B 35. B

SECTION 4 – MATHEMATICS ACHIEVEMENT (PAGES 116-124)

1. B 7. A 13. B 19. A 25. C 31. C 37. D 43. B
2. B 8. C 14. B 20. A 26. B 32. B 38. B 44. D
3. A 9. D 15. B 21. B 27. C 33. D 39. C 45. B
4. B 10. C 16. D 22. D 28. B 34. D 40. C 46. C
5. D 11. C 17. A 23. C 29. A 35. C 41. D 47. A
6. C 12. C 18. D 24. C 30. D 36. B 42. A

SCORING YOUR TEST

On the ISEE, you receive one point for every question you answered correctly, and you receive no points for questions you answered incorrectly or skipped. In each section, the ISEE also includes 5 or 6 experimental questions that do not count towards your score. You won't be told which questions are unscored, and for this reason, these practice tests do not have specific questions marked as experimental. This also means that it isn't possible to determine an exact score for each section of these practice tests, but you can estimate your score using the procedures below.

To estimate your **raw score** for your practice test, first count up the number of questions you answered correctly in each section. Then, follow the table below to subtract 5 or 6 points for each section, accounting for the experimental questions that would not be scored on your actual ISEE exam.

MY RAW SCORE			
Section	**# of Questions Correct**		**Raw Score**
Verbal Reasoning		– 5 =	
Quantitative Reasoning		– 5 =	
Reading Comprehension		– 6 =	
Mathematics Achievement		– 5 =	

SCALED SCORE

Once you have found your raw score, convert it into an approximate **scaled score** using the scoring charts that follow. These charts provide an estimated range for your ISEE scaled score based on your performance on this practice test. Keep in mind that this estimate may differ slightly from your scaled score when you take your actual ISEE exam, depending on the ISEE's specific scaling for that exam and any differences in your own test-taking process.

MIDDLE LEVEL SCALED SCORE RANGES				
Raw Score	**Verbal Reasoning**	**Quantitative Reasoning**	**Reading Comprehension**	**Mathematics Achievement**
42				875 – 905
41				875 – 905
40				870 – 900
39				870 – 900
38				865 – 895
37				865 – 895
36				860 – 890
35	895 – 925			860 – 890
34	890 – 920			855 – 885
33	890 – 920			855 – 885
32	885 – 915	895 – 925		850 – 880
31	885 – 915	895 – 925		850 – 880
30	880 – 910	890 – 920	915 – 940	845 – 875
29	875 – 905	885 – 915	910 – 940	845 – 875
28	875 – 905	885 – 915	905 – 935	845 – 875
27	870 – 900	880 – 910	905 – 935	840 – 870
26	865 – 895	875 – 905	900 – 930	840 – 870
25	865 – 895	875 – 905	895 – 925	835 – 865
24	860 – 890	870 – 900	890 – 920	835 – 865
23	855 – 885	865 – 895	885 – 915	830 – 860
22	855 – 885	865 – 895	885 – 915	830 – 860
21	850 – 880	860 – 890	880 – 910	825 – 855
20	845 – 875	855 – 885	875 – 905	825 – 855

19	845 – 875	855 – 885	870 – 900	820 – 850
18	840 – 870	850 – 880	870 – 900	820 – 850
17	835 – 865	845 – 875	865 – 895	815 – 845
16	835 – 865	845 – 875	860 – 890	815 – 845
15	830 – 860	840 – 870	855 – 885	810 – 840
14	825 – 855	835 – 865	855 – 885	810 – 840
13	825 – 855	835 – 865	850 – 880	805 – 835
12	820 – 850	830 – 860	845 – 875	805 – 835
11	815 – 845	830 – 860	840 – 870	800 – 830
10	815 – 845	825 – 855	835 – 865	800 – 830
9	810 – 840	820 – 850	835 – 865	795 – 825
8	810 – 840	820 – 850	830 – 860	795 – 825
7	805 – 835	815 – 845	825 – 855	790 – 820
6	800 – 830	810 – 840	820 – 850	790 – 820
5	800 – 830	810 – 840	820 – 850	785 – 815
4	795 – 825	805 – 835	815 – 845	785 – 815
3	790 – 820	800 – 830	810 – 840	780 – 810
2	790 – 820	800 – 830	805 – 835	780 – 810
1	785 – 815	795 – 825	805 – 835	775 – 805
0	780 – 810	790 – 820	800 – 830	775 – 805

PERCENTILE

When you take your actual ISEE exam, you will receive a **percentile** ranking comparing your performance against the performance of other students in the same grade who have taken the ISEE that year. For example, a percentile of 62 means that you scored higher than 62% of other ISEE test-takers applying to the same grade. Because your percentile ranking shows how well you performed according to your own grade level, these rankings are frequently given high consideration by admissions offices.

The following charts provide an estimate of your ISEE percentile rankings for this practice test, compared against other students applying to the same grade. For example, if you are scoring at or above the 75th percentile, you are scoring higher than 75% of other ISEE test-takers applying to the same grade. Keep in mind that these percentiles are estimates only, and your actual ISEE percentile will depend on the specific group of students taking the exam in your year.

MIDDLE LEVEL VERBAL REASONING PERCENTILES			
Grade Applying To	**75th percentile**	**50th percentile**	**25th percentile**
Grade 7	880	868	853
Grade 8	890	878	867

MIDDLE LEVEL QUANTITATIVE REASONING PERCENTILES			
Grade Applying To	**75th percentile**	**50th percentile**	**25th percentile**
Grade 7	877	865	853
Grade 8	884	873	864

MIDDLE LEVEL READING COMPREHENSION PERCENTILES			
Grade Applying To	**75th percentile**	**50th percentile**	**25th percentile**
Grade 7	885	869	850
Grade 8	897	883	868

MIDDLE LEVEL MATHEMATICS ACHIEVEMENT PERCENTILES			
Grade Applying To	**75th percentile**	**50th percentile**	**25th percentile**
Grade 7	882	871	861
Grade 8	886	876	867

STANINE

When you receive the score report for your actual ISEE exam, your percentile score will also be broken down into a **stanine**. A stanine is a number from 1-9 obtained by dividing the entire range of students' scores into 9 segments, as shown in the table below:

PERCENTILE RANK	STANINE
1 – 3	1
4 – 10	2
11 – 22	3
23 – 39	4
40 – 59	5
60 – 76	6
77 – 88	7
89 – 95	8
96 – 99	9

Although it isn't possible to calculate your exact stanine from this practice test, you can estimate a stanine score range by looking at your estimated percentile score on each section. For example, if you scored between the 50th and 75th percentile in one of your test sections, your stanine score would be between 5 and 6.